MW00596488

Haunts of
Western Oregon

Haunts of Western Oregon

Kent Goodman

4880 Lower Valley Road, Atglen, Pennsylvania 19310

Ouija is a registered trademark of Parker Brother's Games.
Unless otherwise stated, all artwork photos are by the author.

Other Schiffer Books on Related Subjects:
Ghosts of Portland, Oregon, 978-0-7643-2798-8, $12.95
Greetings from Portland Oregon, 0-7643-2576-0, $24.95

Schiffer Books are available at special discounts for bulk purchases for sales promotions or premiums. Special editions, including personalized covers, corporate imprints, and excerpts can be created in large quantities for special needs. For more information contact the publisher:

Schiffer Publishing Ltd.
4880 Lower Valley Road
Atglen, PA 19310
Phone: (610) 593-1777; Fax: (610) 593-2002
E-mail: Info@schifferbooks.com

For the largest selection of fine reference books on this and related subjects, please visit our web site at **www.schifferbooks.com.** We are always looking for people to write books on new and related subjects. If you have an idea for a book please contact us at the above address.

This book may be purchased from the publisher.Include $5.00 for shipping. Please try your bookstore first. You may write for a free catalog.

In Europe, Schiffer books are distributed by
Bushwood Books
6 Marksbury Ave.
Kew Gardens
Surrey TW9 4JF England
Phone: 44 (0) 20 8392-8585; Fax: 44 (0) 20 8392-9876
E-mail: info@bushwoodbooks.co.uk
Website: www.bushwoodbooks.co.uk
Free postage in the U.K., Europe; air mail at cost.

Copyright © 2009 by Kent Goodman
Library of Congress Control Number: 2008942801

All rights reserved. No part of this work may be reproduced or used in any form or by any means—graphic, electronic, or mechanical, including photocopying or information storage and retrieval systems—without written permission from the publisher.
The scanning, uploading and distribution of this book or any part thereof via the Internet or via any other means without the permission of the publisher is illegal and punishable by law. Please purchase only authorized editions and do not participate in or encourage the electronic piracy of copyrighted materials.
"Schiffer," "Schiffer Publishing Ltd. & Design," and the "Design of pen and ink well" are registered trademarks of Schiffer Publishing Ltd.

Designed by Stephanie Daugherty
Type set in Bard/NewsGoth BT

ISBN: 978-0-7643-3224-1
Printed in United States of America

Dedication

To Terrie, Tom and Noah.
Thanks for believing!

Acknowledgments

First of all, I would like to thank my editor, Dinah Roseberry, for her good-natured, and much needed, pestering, and Jennifer Marie Savage's excellent efforts as my particular editor; secondly I wish to express my gratitude to my good friend Deb McManman for her detailed recollection and first-hand account of a newspaper haunting; thirdly, thanks to the Fountain family for their spooky tales and pictures of Fairview Hospital; fourth, a gracious thanks to the unknown folks who have told me their tales through the Net; and finally, a hearty tip of the hat to whomever is haunting my house right now. *Mi casa es su casa.*

Contents

Contents

Introduction

Welcome

to Haunted Western Oregon

Ghosts linger at the author's home. Here a half-formed human figure can be seen by the light of the porch.

The Willamette Valley is an area of rich farmland that begins south of Portland and is hemmed in by the Cascade Mountains on the east and the Coastal Range on the west. It was the destination that most of the pioneers in the 1840s sacrificed so much to arrive at. As a land filled with deep green forests and many wild areas concealed in mists of fog and drizzle half of the year, it's little wonder that it's home to many stories of hauntings, as well as other strange activity, from the elusive giants of the forests known as Sasquatch to UFOs and monstrous sea serpents patrolling the coast.

Most people in this part of the country consider themselves Oregonians, not tied to one particular locale, and we'll do the same in this book, looking slightly beyond the strict geographical area of the Willamette to include the rocky coastal areas, up some of the local mountains, and as far south as the Klamath caves in our search for the mysterious. To make the search a bit easier, the locations are featured alphabetically.

I have been interested in ghosts and the paranormal since my early teens, and like other true believers, it took a close encounter to cement my faith. I was playing guitar with a friend in a large house built at the turn of the century in Montana. We were sitting around an oak kitchen table that had a large, heavy, silver candleholder in the center. As we talked, the subject of ghosts came up, and I mentioned that I didn't really believe in spirits. At that my friend warned, "You shouldn't say that. The Captain doesn't like people who don't believe in ghosts." As soon as he finished those words, the candleholder slammed sideways onto the table with a force that echoed through the kitchen. That type of proof was enough for me. Since that time I have encountered spirit presences in a number of locations. In fact, the house I live in now is haunted. I often hear sounds of people talking and moving about upstairs when I first enter the house—even though nobody is there. I used to have a mechanical bird that was activated to sing by a motion detector, but I finally had to put it away after it would start warbling in the middle of the night. Similarly, I have a number of Swiss chalet music boxes that play tunes when the lids are open, but many times start playing all by themselves. Another time, a highly skeptical friend was staying at the house in a room where I keep a large cardboard standee of "I Dream of Jeannie." When we met for breakfast I mentioned that he looked as though he hadn't slept a wink. "Of course not," he said with a haunted look, "with that cardboard statue moving around all night!" Even now, a two-year-old staying here stares at a section of the living room, points, and says..."Man!"

What is a ghost? According to some skeptics, a ghost is nothing more than a transient experience of temporal lobe epilepsy. This type of sudden brain malfunction has been proven scientifically to cause the observance of halos, as well as auditory, olfactory, and visual hallucinations. Other feel that instances of sub-audible sound frequencies can also produce paranormal effects, but it should be pointed out that experiments with noise require very large amounts of amplification to achieve results. Considering that around thirty percent of Americans believe in ghosts, can there be that many cases of brain malfunctions or low noises in the country?

Ghosts can be observed in a variety of different ways. Many are felt or heard, like the echo of phantom footsteps; some can be smelled, as in the case of a departed ones' favorite pipe tobacco or perfume that still lingers in the home. Of the types that can be seen, a majority appear to be performing some action over and over. In a way, these apparitions are like paranormal videotapes that keep rewinding to a certain scene. When a person dies suddenly as a result of tragic circumstances, the energy around that event is sometimes strong enough to "stick" it in a certain place and time, to be witnessed for years afterwards. Some of these entities, instead of having a sad tale to tell, are just repeating the same comforting motions that they performed while alive. They may not realize that they're no longer living, or that the location of buildings have changed, which is why they can often be seen walking through walls or trodding on a sunken floor that is no longer there. This goes on for many years because, after all, time is just a relative term used here on Earth as it travels around the sun. That sort of time has no meaning on the Other Side, so something that occurred twenty, or even fifty years ago, was just the other day for them. Other types of spirits are quite aware of their surroundings and often hang around a home or building that has had an effect on them when living. In other words, they like to keep an eye on things, and are very unappreciative of any structural changes to their surroundings. Some spirits are helpful and comforting while fortunately only a few seem to have a malevolent intent.

Ghosts are more often seen at night, perhaps because their ethereal nature makes them hard to see during the glare of the daylight. It might also have something to do with our other senses, especially our basic, primal ones being more attuned at night when we can't rely on sight. In fact, ghosts can be thought of as a form of telepathic communication. They are seen in your mind if it's open, which is why many children and some attuned adults see spirits when others can't. This is also why I believe there are very few actual photos of ghosts. Most supposed spirit photos can be explained as bugs, dust particles, fog, and reflections. In other words, if ghosts communicate themselves to observers through some sort of mental imagery, it's no wonder there aren't many bona fide spirit pictures. It's very hard to take a photo of a thought! According to some psychics that I have spoken with who use this same type of energy, the presence of harsh light can cause actual burning to the spirits (and psychics) unless subdued lighting is used.

Spirit presences can be felt in rooms because of a drop in temperature and in many cases, electronic equipment will malfunction. These are caused by the spirits, who somehow use whatever energy is in the area in order to manifest. This is also why observers can find themselves feeling drained of energy after an encounter. With more and better technology comes the chance to interact with ghosts on a more complete level. For instance, by using simple tape recorders, researchers have managed to ask questions of a spirit and get direct answers that will later appear on the tape, even if they are unheard at the time. Perhaps some day we will perfect the technology enough so that anyone could converse with the Other World. But would we want to? Why would we want to? To conquer our fear of the ultimate unknown? Once that door is open, could it be closed again? Are some things best left sleeping?

I believe the spirit world and our world exist in the same area, but we are unaware of each other for the most part. A good analogy is that of an ant. You can go out in the yard and watch an ant as it busily goes about its daily life, rushing here and there, picking up leaves, feeding the kids, fending off other bugs. So busy, and their time on earth is so short. We live in exactly the same area as they do, but we remain completely oblivious to them. We have different concerns. Our life and timetables aren't on the same wavelength. We only interact with each other on rare occasions when our paths cross, such as when we stand on an anthill.

The important thing to remember is, there *is* another world out there: A world of flying saucers, ghosts, monsters, fairies, and energies — a world that was magical once. It can be exciting to take a quick peek at it now and then.

This book only brushes the tip of the iceberg. Most people experiencing ghosts or anything else paranormal keep it to themselves for fear of ridicule. I have found when researching this book that most people will immediately laugh at the idea of spirits and the supernatural, but when they find that I am genuine in my interest and am not looking to make them appear foolish, will more often than not relate a ghost story of their own. I'm always interested in hearing from anyone with a story to tell. Please write to me at:

kgoodman@amselmedia.com

or Kent Goodman,

P.O. Box 21038,

Eugene, OR 97402

Many people are visiting psychics now to try to interact with loved ones. I agree with the psychics who all state: Don't wait until a person is a ghost to make amends or to tell them how you feel. It's much easier to do it in the here and now.

Kent Goodman, Eugene, Oregon, 2008

Miscellaneous Spooks

The following encounters with ghostly and paranormal entities are arranged alphabetically by town to make tracking down the elusive beings a bit easier. However, some ghosts and/or legends have a habit of moving around a large area —

the whole subject area of this book, for example. Instead of including the same items over and over, I have included these Wholly Roaming Vapors here. All of them feature in more than one location, often with very slight deviations in appearance. Are they actual sightings, or are they stories conjured up in a darkened room? To be sure, many come complete with lurid descriptions of appearances quite out of the ordinary, for instance, the old lady who casually drinks gasoline from a pump, the man walking around with an axe in his head, or the lady with hair on fire. These seem like the subjects of horror films, or perhaps actual sightings that get better with each retelling. Who knows what otherworldly presence can be found when you're walking along a lonely stretch of road late on a rain-soaked night? Maybe one of these Oregonian shades:

🍂 A woman with worms crawling out of her eye sockets, usually seen in a car.

🍂 A man with no head riding a motorcycle on a dark road. He vanishes as soon as someone notices him.

🍂 A lumberjack carrying a large axe can sometimes be seen looking into the windows of houses late at night. Not to be confused with the ghost of a young air force pilot who spies on people through an air vent. Or the young cowboy who stares at people sleeping in bed.

🍂 Sometimes a headless woman can be seen when you look in the bathroom mirror of certain homes.

🍂 Another late night being is that of a bat that turns itself into a vampire and walks from house to house.

🍂 The apparition of a woman who has both her head and arms cut off can be observed wandering the streets around midnight. Aimlessly, you would think.

🍂 A young woman who has a rope tied around her neck can be seen in certain towns.

🍂 Incredibly, the ghost of a woman engulfed in fire, and yet still carrying a gasoline tank, can be witnessed picking flowers in the front yard of a house. Now that's (un)living dangerously!

🍂 The spectre of an old lady carrying a rifle can be observed standing in the street in some towns. Maybe she had something to do with the ghost of a man with a large hole in his torso who can be seen smoking a pipe.

🍂 Of course there's always the skeleton that can be seen sitting at the dinner table.

🍂 The ghost of a woman mailing a letter at the post office is a little unusual, but the fact that she had an axe sticking out of her head makes the sight more memorable still.

🍂 The ghost of a coal miner (or in some cases, an Indian chief) has been witnessed running after cars on a dark road late at night. Sometimes a strange creature has also been sighted, looking in the grass for something along the highway.

🍂 The ghost of a young man dressed in a leather jacket has been witnessed on numerous occasions, walking a dog late at night on a dark Eugene street.

Ghosts and spooks don't have to obey the same physical laws that we mortals do. A thirsty spirit takes a nice drink from a gas hose.

🍂 The ghost of an old lady can be seen doing something pretty dangerous — drinking gasoline from a pump at an old gas station.

🍂 A Civil War soldier can sometimes be witnessed hitch-hiking along dark roads.

🍂 A ship's captain can be seen throwing rocks in one town.

🍂 A railroad engineer can be seen casually sitting outside on a porch in a couple of towns.

- The spirit of a street bum can be seen drinking blood from a beaker.

- A pregnant woman appeared talking into thin air as if someone else was there. Being frightened by the onlookers the ghost made it's way into the dark.

- A man with the head of a goblin has been seen dragging a body through a park—another good reason not to hang out in parks late at night.

- An old prospector with a wooden leg (named Smith?) is sometimes witnessed digging through garbage cans.

An odd sighting of an ogre dragging away a lifeless body.

A nurse with a bloody uniform can often be seen watching TV in a living room late at night.

A ghost is sometimes witnessed hovering in the air like a balloon.

A flight attendant has been seen on a few occasions going through the refrigerator in the kitchen of a home in the early morning hours.

A badly mangled hunter dragging a dead bear appeared in a house. The ghost did not appear to be bothered by the onlookers.

A phantom mailman has been seen on a few occasions by a man camping outside of different towns.

A man dressed as janitor is sometimes witnessed in a college dorm.

An airline pilot talks to someone who isn't visible.

A woman with worms crawling out of her eye sockets can be seen riding a horse.

A coal miner sometimes walks through a local house.

A young cowboy can be seen raiding the refrigerator.

A Civil War-era ghost can be seen in the mirror in a local house.

🍂 On a scarier note, there is a partially decomposed body that looks at people through the air vent in a house.

🍂 The ghost of a nurse in a bloody uniform can be seen mailing a letter. And speaking of mail, a mailman has been seen answering a call at a payphone.

🍂 The same goes for the spirit of a cleaning woman who can be seen just outside of town in certain areas. How do we know she's a cleaning woman? Does she carry a mop? Who knows?

🍂 Continuing on the road theme, a military man can be observed hitchhiking. And a pregnant lady can sometimes be seen in the backseat if you drive through the area.

🍂 Another lady, covered in blood, stands right in the middle of the road. A frequent visitor to many areas is a flight attendant who rides a motorcycle.

🍂 If you go off the beaten path, or street, the ghosts get scarier. A lumberjack with a large axe has been reported at a number of area campgrounds. In a deserted area is a female ghost with a goat's head.

Chapter One

Apparitions Abound

Albany

One of the more unusual sightings near the town of Albany occurred at Conseur Lake. It was there that witnesses have reported seeing a monster that looked a lot like Bigfoot—except it had white hair, pointed cat-like ears, and webbed feet.

According to a series of articles written in the now-defunct newspaper Greater Oregon, locals in the area told of a UFO that had crashed, and before long, sightings of the eight-foot monster began to circulate. Soon, hundreds of people from all over were combing the area, armed with rifles, ready to bag an alien.

A psychic apparently contacted it, and found out that it was an alien, with the cute name of Flix. He said he felt very lonely. Poor monster! Even so, locals started taking potshots at him until public outrage made them stop.

According to a number of websites, in the town itself, there were some strange goings-on at the Hereford Steer Restaurant. The owner of the eatery was killed, mistakenly it seems, by the police inside the restaurant. As often happens, sudden

A silver-haired alien with the cuddly name of Flix was seen in the Albany area.

violent deaths tend to create ghosts, and sure enough, it wasn't long before pictures were being turned upside down, candles on the tables were snuffed out, hats were flipped off employees' heads, and sometimes entire meals were sent flying to the floor. Does it sound like an exciting place to eat? Unfortunately, it was torn down a number of years ago.

Not all ghosts are creepy. Sometimes it depends on your point of view. For instance, one lady in town prefers to think of her house *not* as haunted, but as 'inhabited'. Her ghost gave her a helping hand once when she lost her balance on a ladder. She was at the point of falling…when she felt two large hands gently push her back up.

The entity also comforts her dog that was abused in the past. At night she has seen *him* on her bed, wearing a long dark coat and wide brim hat (she calls him The Preacher) petting the frightened pooch to calm it down. When she has thanked him out loud, he looks up startled...*and disappears*.

Alsea

Keep your eyes peeled if you happen to be walking along the streets of Alsea at night. You might see the ghost of a teenage girl walking a dog, or a man with the head of a pig (related to the goat-headed ghost of Albany?), or possibly the headless man who rummages through garbage cans. A more run-of-the-mill ghost is that of a policeman who appears watching television in his living room.

Ashland

There is only one famous ghost in this area of Oregon. Not famous for being a spirit, but famous in his own right — the actor Charles Laughton. Although he appeared in many movies, Laughton always had his heart set on playing the role of either "King Lear" or "Falstaff" at Ashland's renowned Shakespeare Theatre. One year he finally had the opportunity to do so, but, unfortunately, he suddenly died before his wish could be fulfilled.

Simply dying was not going to keep the great thespian from pursuing his dream though, and so he haunts the Elizabethan Theatre, where he has been seen in full Falstaff costume. He can also be heard laughing in the audience during performances and singing at night.

The theatre has made Ashland famous, but the beautiful Lithia Park, located right downtown, is also a major attraction for tourists—*and ghosts*. The most well known is that of the

The actor Charles Laughton had always wanted to play Falstaff at Ashland's Shakespeare Theatre, but died before getting the chance. He can be seen in full costume at the venue.

Dog-Faced Boy, a child who lived in the area during the 1920s and had the double misfortune of being hunchbacked and hairy all over his body because of a medical condition. The poor soul had to survive as best he could by selling pencils and sometimes stealing small things and hiding them in his ever-present gunnysack. In 1926 he disappeared, most likely murdered. However, in the 1960s he started to be frequently seen wandering the park. The police were called, but he always disappeared before they arrived. Were they chasing a ghost?

The park is also home to a logger who was killed in an accident. His presence is known by the unmistakable smell of Lithia water that he drank so much of. He is joined by the spirit of a girl who was raped and murdered in the park during the late 1800s. She can be seen as a blue mist that rises gently over the center of the pond in the park.

Perhaps anything with the word "Lithia" in its name is haunted. It's certainly the case of the Ashland Spring Hotel, formerly known as Lithia Springs Hotel. When it opened in 1925, it was the tallest building between San Francisco and Portland. Wealthy clients came from far and wide to take in the mineral waters, but when the train line closed, the guests stopped and the hotel closed in the late 1990s. It was reopened a number of years ago and even though no cost was spared in its refurbishment, it still just looks haunted. And, not all of its previous guests have left, either. There is the ghost of a boy who can be seen, along with shadowy figures at night, and a strange presence in Room 517.

Southern Oregon University

Ashland is also home to Southern Oregon University, noted for a number of hauntings.

Plunkett Center witnessed a scary séance in the 1970s, when calling forth beings from the other side had terrifying results. A professor and three studentsheld the seance in one of the upper floors of the building, using a Ouija board. At one point, the board jumped into the air, sending the terrified group running into the street.

The basement of Suzanne Holmes dormitory is haunted by a little boy who drowned in the water that accumulated when the place was being built.

Churchill Hall is the oldest building on the site and at one time a group of students were practicing in the auditorium. As the evening wore on, it began to get dark and someone shouted for the lights to be turned on. They immediately were, which was great until the students realized that the light room was locked and empty. Suddenly, everyone had a good reason to leave in a hurry. In the same building it was known that if you swore, something would pull your hair. A bit more spine tingling was the eerie gobbling sound and the putrid smell of rotting meat experienced by one student as he cleaned around a curtain. Sounds like a zombie turkey now, but when it occurred it must have been truly frightening.

There was once a person who was walking through Taylor Hall and saw a close friend of his. The friend said he had to run an errand, but would be right back. However, he never returned. The friend, a security guard at the hall, had died of a heart attack at the same moment he spoke with the other person. To say he never came back isn't quite true. He never came back *alive*, but he roams the halls still. For instance, one lady who worked at the hall had a habit of locking her office door every time she left. Once, she realized that she had left her purse locked in her room, and was just about to call security when an older security guard, dressed in a blue uniform, asked if she needed help and then proceeded to unlock her door. It was only later when she remembered that all the security guards wear gray or brown uniforms that the mysterious man, while completely real appearing, was not altogether here. The blue uniforms hadn't been used in twenty years.

Maybe that guard liked helping women. Maybe Jon, a student there, got on his nerves. For instance, one time Jon was going through some gold boxes he had found and came upon a photo of the phantom guard when he was alive. In the shot, the man was proudly holding the diploma he had received in criminal justice.

At that moment, Jon felt someone standing behind him and saw that it was the person in the photo, only older and definitely not smiling. He told Jon to stop rummaging around before someone got hurt and to leave the building. In another instance, Jon was cleaning up after a meeting and went to return some materials to the storage area in the basement next to the boiler room. When he arrived he saw the shadow cast by a person walking around in the room and when he opened the door, the guard was there, who sent him packing once again.

Another campus building that is chock full of ghosts is Britt Hall. The most obvious is the ghost of an old janitor who had worked there. When he was alive, he made a nuisance of himself to the girls and boys with his roaming hands and rushing fingers. Now you can still smell the stinky old letch, especially on the second floor, where his raspy breathing echoes in the hall and his hands are always trying to touch some hapless student. He's not the only one visiting from the *other side*, though. The spirit of a soldier can be seen walking down a hall, visible only from the waist up, and in the theatre there's a phantom who can often be seen in the projection booth. What is it with ghosts and their fascination with light and sound booths? Were they all in the AV Club before death?

A house on Windsor Street near the University was haunted. In the early 1980s the house was only ten years old, and yet when Kim, a co-ed at the school, was doing her homework, she would sometimes feel such a malevolent energy that she knew she had to get out of the house quickly or die. She would run outside no matter what the weather, even into snowstorms, and wait until the energy dissipated. The poltergeist activity included hiding clothes and, on one occasion, a book that had just been left for a minute was gone for good. Her scariest encounter happened when she was alone in the house. She was reading in an upstairs room when she heard the door open and footsteps echoing up the stairs. She assumed robbers were in the house until she saw the shadow of an old lady in a calf-length dress, sweater, and clunky shoes walking up the stairs. The lady's hand was on the rail, and as she stepped onto the landing she saw Kim. The ghost jumped in surprise and ran off around the corner into another room.

Aumsville

I had never heard of the small town of Aumsville, but it seems to be pretty popular with those souls who are presently between lives. The list of ghosts and spirits include:

- A young woman walking the hallways of the local high school.

- A lady who carries her head under her arm has been seen staring at a person sleeping in a bed while a lady with *no* head at all can be seen playing a piano in a different house. Another female ghost is that of a young girl in a bloody prom dress searching for something under parked cars.

- Someone dressed like a ship's captain snoops through mailboxes late at night.

- An army uniform was seen crawling out of a manhole. *Yes, just the uniform*. The witness ran away. Wouldn't you?

- Ghosts in this area have a shoe fixation. For instance, a man carrying a sword has been seen trying on shoes in a local house, as has a partially decomposed person.

- One of the more unusual ghosts is that of a woman with a knife in her chest; she floats in the air like a balloon.

In line with other weird sightings, a lady can be seen playing piano. Without her head.

🍁 The college has at least two ghosts, one with a skeleton face and the other a janitor who is seen fairly often.

🍁 Another active ghost has been seen elsewhere, the old prospector with the wooden leg. This time he's seen digging through garbage cans.

Chapter Two

Back-Bending Spirits

Baker City

This town has one well-known haunted house. Actually, it's more than a house; it's the Geiser Grand Hotel that was first opened in 1889 during the Gold Rush. The lavish building featured everything that money could buy, including crystal chandeliers and even a two hundred-foot corner cupola. However, like most Gold Rush buildings, it fell on hard times after the boom was over, and finally closed for good in 1968. New owners spent $6 million restoring the grand building, and it reopened in 1999.

One thing that most ghost researchers agree on is that restoration work is a sure way to *awaken* spirits—and that's just what happened. The lock on the door of the cupola never worked, almost as if the spirits were keeping that one for themselves. When the owner entered the room on one occasion, everything in it had been turned upside down. A lady in blue grandly descends the main staircase, and flapper girls can be seen watching from the second floor balustrade. Loud parties can be heard still raving on empty floors. At the Geiser, it seems like the fun never stops.

Bend

Situated in the high desert region in the Cascades, this is one of Oregon's fastest growing areas. It's popular

A friendly mountain man has been seen in a private house. He is well-liked and welcome to stay.

with everyone, from ski bums to multi-millionaires…*and a few ghosts as well.* The spirits that still live in Bend are mostly of the smoke and footsteps variety, although one house in town featured a room that was haunted by a lady who previously lived there. According to a local author, the daughter of the new owners commented that a misty shape could be seen in one end of the room, and at times a dark-haired woman would sit on the corner of her bed and talk with her. She was also seen pacing back and forth in front of the window and wringing her hands in anguish. After a number of years, the sightings occurred with less frequency, and a psychic now states that the spirit has found her way in the next world.

A mountain man, dressed in all the trimmings—wide brimmed hat, checkered shirt, thick boots—can be seen visiting many different rooms in a private house near Brooks Scanlon Mill. He's friendly and well liked, so nobody minds him being there.

The O'Kane Building and the old Mt. View Hospital both feature the wispy smoke trails of ghosts, along with footsteps, voices, and creaking floors. If that's not spooky enough, locals go to the old smoke stacks at night, where it's said that ghosts walk around and move things. What is it with ghosts and moving things? Bored, or just tidy?

The Elks Lodge in town is haunted by a distinguished-looking spirit who arrives after large functions. He's heard first, walking up the stairs into the building from outside, and then can be seen walking across a hallway.

Brownsville

The hauntings in this area are mostly of the local legend type. For instance:

❧ A badly burned woman has been seen walking through a house;

❧ A young Indian warrior has also been seen wandering through the graveyard;

❧ A female ghost has been observed making a call at a pay phone;

❧ Somewhat harder to believe is the black cat that turns into a woman who searches for a lost item on the ground.

Chapter Three

Cosmic Happenings

Cannon Beach

For some reason, this pleasant town on the Pacific coast has some of the most exciting hair-raising hauntings around.

Ecola State Park, situated close to the town, was the site for an uncanny encounter. A number of people have seen a couple strolling hand-in-hand on the trail close to Indian Beach. In one memorable incident, two people saw the couple walking ahead of them on the narrow trail, and were even given the time of day by the phantom pair. The witnesses watched the couple disappear around a bend in the trail, but when they came to the same area a minute later, the first couple had vanished. The area in question has washed away, and the trail ends at a cliff face—there was no place the ghostly couple could have gone.

The Warren House, a restaurant in Cannon Beach, is also home to spooks. A ghostly presence was enough to give a hardy cook goose bumps, make all his hair stand on end, and drain the color from his face. In another instance, a man was seen walking out of the restaurant's bathroom although only the observer and the cook were in the building at the time.

A Ghost or A Mummy?

Undoubtedly, one of Oregon's spookiest ghost legends is that of Cannon Beach's Bandage Man. The story tells of a person,

One of the most terrifying ghosts in Oregon is Bandage Man, who tries to strangle drivers and has even been seen carrying a body over his shoulder.

possibly a logger, who had been in a horrific accident and was covered in bandages. Whether he's alive or is a ghost, no one is sure, but he is known to live in the area of an old quarry that lies at the end of a long-disused section of highway. On certain nights, especially when the coastal area is filled with thick fog, he jumps into the backs of trucks traveling the off-ramp into town. He then rails and smashes at the windows, roof, and doors of the vehicle, terrifying the drivers. By the time the driver pulls into town, Bandage Man has disappeared, although he often leaves his calling card behind — foul-smelling, bloody bandages.

The Bandage Man story started to circulate a few days after reports about an injured giant escaping from an ambulance surfaced. One local man told of his own scary encounter that occurred late at night. He had pulled off the highway and was driving along the exit ramp when his truck started to shake violently, which he assumed was caused by the wind. He was more concerned about the fuel level in his truck, but as he turned on the cab lights to get a better look, he was startled to see a giant mummy staring at him from the rear-view mirror. He was still trying to think of a logical explanation (maybe someone was playing a prank?) when he felt a huge crash as the rear window was knocked out and the mummy was reaching in, trying to grab his neck! The horrific giant furiously continued to swipe at his neck as the driver careened into town. As soon as his truck hit the main street, the mummy suddenly let go and disappeared into the night.

On another occasion a driver on the highway outside of town noticed a hitchhiker along the road. Looking in his rearview mirror, he was shocked and terrified to see the giant Bandage Man walk up silently behind the hitchhiker, bash him on the head, and then sling him over his shoulder like a sack of potatoes, before walking over the edge of the street into the brush.

Hitchhikers and truck drivers weren't the only living things that had to be careful. A local legend recounts a time in the winter of 1979 when many of the local dogs began to disappear. It was one of the coldest seasons on record with a scarcity of food being one of the side effects. Often, in the area where the dogs went missing, rotten bandages were found, and the locals knew just who to blame. According to the story, on one particularly bitter night, complete with driving rain and howling wind, an old local man named Emmett and his dog Maude were relaxing in the comfort of their cabin when the dog started to bark furiously at the window. The more Emmett tried to calm the terrified animal, the more it barked, its hair standing on end. Finally, the man decided to have a closer look outside, but just as he approached the window, it exploded into hundreds of shards. To his horror, Emmett watched as a giant bandaged arm reached in and grabbed the unfortunate dog. He immediately grabbed his shotgun and fired two shells into the giant at point blank range, but the monster simply turned and walked into the dark night with its trophy.

Cave Junction

There is a tragic story associated with Room 308 in Oregon Caves Lodge, which is situated next to the Oregon Caves, a frequent location for Sasquatch sightings. A young couple honeymooned there a number of years ago, and one day, when the wife came back from a walk unexpectedly, she found her new husband in bed with the maid. Overcome with grief, she slit her wrists that very evening, and ever since then has caused trouble for maids working in that room. When the sheets and towels have been folded, the maids can't leave the room even for a second, because if they do, the laundry will be scattered all around the room. Visitors staying in the room often hear footsteps in the hall and can feel an eerie presence.

Coos Bay

You would think psychic people would have a history with ghosts, and according to a psychic named Heather, it's true. Heather tells me that she and her brother have always been psychic and are trying to form a ghost-hunting group in Eugene. Here is a story from Coos Bay on the Oregon coast:

I used to live in a really old house. I was fourteen and a lot happened there—apparitions, stuff disappearing, footsteps, and even a ghost who saved me one night.

We moved into the house when I was fourteen. It was built in the 1930s and was kind of creepy from the outside already. It was two stories, but we were only allowed to use the bottom half, as the upstairs was all torn up. From where we were there was a door from our living room leading out into a mudroom and the front door. In the mudroom there were stairs leading up into the top of the home. I was unloading boxes in what was to be my room, and right under the stairs leading to the top floor, I started to feel cold, so I put a sweater on. The next thing I saw was a wrapped up extension cord that jumped from the box onto the floor next to me. That did freak me out a bit, but I had been around this stuff all my life, so I just went about the business of setting up my new room. As time went by, I began hearing footsteps going up and down the stairs at night even though both my parents and my brother were sleeping. There were knocks on the ceiling and other strange noises that could not be explained. Once, my step-dad swore he heard someone say his name, and whenever I had friends over to stay the night, we could always hear noises upstairs, and nonchalantly I would say, "It's just the ghost."

Chapter Three: Cosmic Happenings

The night a ghost helped me was one I will never forget. My parents were heavy drinkers, and sometimes they would fight, scream, and even hit each other. This was one of those nights, and I was lying on the couch with my pillow over my head to drown them out. The next thing I knew my step-dad had my mother in a headlock and I began yelling for him to let her go. They were right in front of the mudroom door, and there was a loud bang on the outside of the door, like something was thrown against it. My step-dad opened the door, looked out, and saw that there was nothing there. Nothing had hit it, or fell against it. The front door was locked, and no one was upstairs... but the fighting stopped. And I was grateful.

Corvallis

The town of Corvallis is most well known for its school, Oregon State University. However, it's the lower form schools that get the ghosts.

At Cheldelin Middle School, a janitor died while at work, and now, even when the doors are locked, he can be heard going about his duties, whistling and keys jingling as he pushes his broom across the empty halls.

At Crescent Valley High School it's the theatre that's haunted. On stage you can feel strange drafts, the curtains billow, and chairs move across the stage by themselves. In addition, the costume room features a cold, unwelcoming presence and the costumes themselves have been known to move from place to place.

The University does get credit for one haunting—that of Room 121 in Sackett Hall Dormitory. During the 1950s, a girl had been killed there, either accidentally or on purpose. In either case, now objects move around and mysterious fires have a habit of starting in the building.

Room 121 in Sackett Hall on the Oregon State University campus is haunted by the spirit of a girl who was killed there, possibly even murdered.

The janitor at Cheldelin Middle School can be heard whistling while he works, even though he has already died.

Camp Adair outside of Corvallis was used as a Prisoner of War camp during the Second World War. A number of them died in the infirmary there and, according to reports, the souls of the German and Italian prisoners still haunt the halls.

Miscellaneous ghosts around town include a cowboy who stares at people sleeping in their beds and a young woman covered in blood who plays the piano.

Cottage Grove

There appears to be a wide variety of ghosts and spirits in this small town.

At Roger's Paint and Body Repair you can hear heavy footsteps going up and down the stairs, feel a presence, and of course, tools get moved around. The place is still open, operating under a new name, but the owners just as soon not discuss the ghostly happenings that occur there.

✿ On the upper floor of a group of buildings on Main Street, above the Book Mine, loud parties, talking, and footsteps can often be heard coming from the empty premises. Concerned storeowners have gone up to the rooms to stop the partying to find themselves alone in an empty room.

✿ Something strange is also happening on nearby Mt. David. Certain rock features of this mountain were sacred to the local Kalapuya Indians, who held large ceremonies near them in which they re-enacted their creation myths. Perhaps they have someone permanently on guard, because, according to lcoal lore and websites, there is some sort of spirit that will chase the unwary off the mountain if they venture there at night.

✿ Other reports include a man carrying a bloody axe, the ghost of a security guard with a bullet hole in his forehead, a lady with a blue face, and the ghost of an old man with a long white beard.

Creswell

A small town with a small amount of ghost sightings, including a badly mangled hunter dragging a dead bear and a headless man riding a horse along a highway, apparently seeking revenge for his murder.

Chapter Four

Eugene

There are a fair number of ghosts present in Eugene, which makes sense as it's the largest town between San Francisco and Portland and home of the University of Oregon. A large percentage of the area's spirits are active in the schools with only just a couple doing their bit "off campus."

The most famous local haunting is the one at South Eugene High School. It's so well known that we even know the name of the ghost — Robert Granke. Apparently Robert, a student, was high up in the catwalks above the stage in the school's auditorium during the late 1950s when he fell to his death in the seats below. Ever since then, the auditorium has been haunted, and there's even a Robert Granke chair that not many people feel like sitting in. He can be heard walking around and can sometimes be seen as a shadowy form in the balcony.

Once, a theatre teacher chased what he thought was a student in a white shirt through the catwalk. It was stuffy, dangerous, and very claustrophobic in the narrow confines, and it seemed like the student was always just out of reach. Finally, the instructor knew he had him cornered as they came to a brick wall. However, the "student" simply passed right *through* it. The teacher made it to the stage floor in record time after the encounter.

The auditorium at South Eugene High School is where student Robert Granke met his untimely death, and where his shadowy form can still be seen.

Fox Hollow Elementary School has its own ghost: a young person called Opal who has been seen many times. When the area gets dark at night, witnesses have heard a voice calling the name "Opal" again and again. Whoever the child is, its presence can be seen on the playground equipment as it shakes and bends...even when there is no one there.

Lane Community College also has a haunted area—the elevator in the center building on campus. It was in this same elevator shaft that a janitor fell to his death in the 1960s. At sunset his pitiful cries for help can be heard, and he sometimes likes to take passengers for an unexpected ride into the dim and spooky basement. Aren't basements always spooky? This one just may be a little more so than the norm.

Pocket Theatre, located in the basement of one of the oldest buildings on the University of Oregon campus, is reputed to be haunted. The tiny space is already very small and cramped, and it doesn't take much imagination to feel a presence there—and many theatre students do *feel* a presence.

Room 101 in Stafford Hall (a residence hall) holds an attraction for a dark male figure that can be seen peering into the windows or darting around corners. However, he is most often seen standing across from Pioneer Cemetery, which is located a short distance away from the building. He only appears late at night when the campus is very quiet.

Another ghost sighting at the cemetery happened in the 1970s when three friends were walking across the area close to midnight. As they walked, one of the friends suddenly stopped

Eugene's Pioneer Cemetery, located next to the University of Oregon's campus, has been the focal point for various apparitions, including a lady in white and a bagpiper in full regalia.

and stared with a look of absolute shock on his face. The others followed his gaze and saw a woman in a long, flowing white wedding dress. Unusually, her head was about fifteen feet off the ground, with the area under her feet covered in a thick fog—even though there was a complete absence of any kind of fog elsewhere. The friends looked at each other, but when they turned to look back, the apparition had vanished.

A few weeks later, next to the graveyard, a student was crossing a field again late at night and was surprised to hear the plaintive skirl of a bagpipe. As he turned toward the sound, he saw a tall man in full Black Watch regalia slowly marching toward him, playing a mournful tune on the pipe. As the ghostly piper neared, another group of students appeared and suddenly the piper was gone. Did this otherworldly sentry guard the sacred grounds, or is the piper himself one of the many bodies that have rested here for generations?

A few of the area's grand homes are reputed to harbor spirits, including the Victorian Shelton-McMurphy-Johnson House and the Campbell House; the latter is now an inn. Both residences have had their share of ghostly footsteps and unseen presences. Certain rooms also have an undeniable unwelcoming feeling.

In one apartment building downtown, one of the tenants often hears the radio turn on in the living room around 3 o'clock in the morning. He gets up, walks into the room, and sits down to listen to music for twenty minutes or so *with* an older gentleman sitting in the easy chair. He's the previous owner who died a few years before. After awhile, he slowly disappears.

Another case of ghosts in the house concerns a possessed china cabinet. According to family members, if you looked in the china cabinet, you would not only feel a presence, but could clearly see the reflection of the family's deceased grandmother.

Woodland Park is where a young boy was shot while on the playground. If you visit there after midnight, he might approach you and warn you to leave.

The town's art cinema, the Bijou, is also reported to have spiritual rumblings, perhaps because it served as a mortuary for many years. There are two other rather unlikely places for ghosts, but they seem to stand up to some scrutiny.

The K-Mart store once featured an auto service center that is now closed. However, an unseen but clearly felt presence is there. In addition, night workers tell of doors opening and closing by themselves, signs moving of the own accord, and on one frightening night a ten-foot section of "Talking Elmo" dolls that all started chattering away at once...even though they weren't sound activated. The Toys R Us store has the same problem in the upstairs section of their warehouse. Boxes have been thrown, all the lights go out, walkie-talkies suddenly go silent...in fact, workers will only go in using the buddy system because of the weird phantom activity.

On more of a domestic note, a couple of sisters found a house to rent at an unreasonably cheap price, and being students at the university, they jumped at the opportunity. The building was actually a guest house behind one of the bigger houses located on one of the town's main streets. It seemed very cute and pleasant, but it only took one day to see why the rent was so cheap.

Strange, unnerving sounds could be heard, like the crying of a child outside, or footsteps going up the stairs. These could have been the result of over-active imaginations, but bigger things were in store. Once, the pair woke up in the middle of the night to find that all of their furniture had been rearranged, completely silently. Another time, one of the women could feel

The Shelton-McMurphy-Johnson house has, like other Victorian residences, unseen presences, footsteps and forbidding rooms.

someone walking behind them, and when she turned around, the wet footprints of a young child could be seen on the floor. The other sister got the scare of her life when she felt someone push her while she was washing her hair in the bathroom. Then the door locked and she felt the heavy presence of evil in the small room. She finally broke the window and escaped outside. They immediately broke their lease and found another place to stay. The landlord admitted that he knew the place was haunted.

Chapter Four: Eugene

Another haunted house was also located just off campus. A man noticed that one of his roommates had left the lights on in his room all through the night, and in the morning he went to check on him. The roommate said that during the night he smelled cigarette smoke and turned on his lights to make sure a dangerous stub wasn't smoldering somewhere. To his surprise and horror, he saw a very old lady sitting on a trunk at the foot of his bed, smoking. She stared at him balefully with an ugly face full of malice, and the man couldn't do anything except quietly return the stare until he finally was so exhausted he fell asleep.

Ghost wants in! Nothing like hearing metal slamming against your door to wake you up in a real hurry. But that's just what happened to one man in Eugene as he lay in his bed reading. He heard a loud 'splang' noise that sounded like metal being bent hard and springing back, as if someone was trying to pry the door open. He shot out of bed to check the area, but nothing was out of the ordinary. However, no sooner had he returned to his reading when he heard the sounds of his bedroom door being smashed against the frame, not once, but many times, gaining in intensity as whatever it was tried to bust in. Needless to say, like any brave ghost-hunter, he hid under the blankets until it stopped (wouldn't we all?).

The road between Eugene and the next town to the west, Veneta, is pretty much straight and smooth, and yet people have been killed in car crashes in the area. One accident had left a man dead, and two months after the event, a woman who was driving along the same stretch of road where the accident occurred was shocked to see a man climb out of a ditch and walk directly in front of her. It was too late to brake and, as she drove *through* the person, she immediately recognized the image to be that of the dead man, which had been broadcast on the news.

Chapter Five

Fighting Ghosts

Forest Grove

A phantom bugler would travel around the area, blowing on his bugle that made a low sound, not much different from the noise trees make. One day a cougar attacked the huge bugler. He killed the beast using his favorite musical instrument, his bugle, but lay in the road for two days and nights, unable to move because of loss of blood.

The mangled man finally made his way back to his cabin where he died of his wounds. Since then, only one person has seen him. He was walking along when the bugler stood and blocked the path. The phantom had huge scars on his face as a result of the cougar fight and was in a very bad temper. He raised his bugle high and swung at the hapless onlooker with enough force to crush his skull. The man quickly ducked and ran away. This happened nearly a hundred years ago, and every once in a while a person is found dead in the woods, his head crushed by the blow of a bugle.

A phantom bugler who bears the scars of a fight with a cougar haunts the woods near here, and will smash the head of anyone unfortunate enough to come close to his instrument.

Heceta Head Lighthouse is one of the most photographed lighthouses in the country.

Florence

Heceta Head Lighthouse, located a few miles north of Florence, is one of the most photographed lighthouses in the country. Perched atop a hill overlooking the gray Pacific Ocean, it's in the perfect spot. The building was first put to use in 1894 with a light that was visible for many miles out to sea. The lighthouse is now electronic and run remotely by the Coast Guard, and the only original building left besides it is the picturesque white caretaker's house, built in the Queen Anne style. The house is so nice that at least one former resident has *never* left it. Visitors to the home have witnessed the ghost of a little old lady who rattles the dishes, walks through doors, makes frightening noises, and in general keeps an eye on the house. Her name is Rue.

At least, that's the name that came up on a Ouija® board one night. A local tradition states that she is the unhappy wife

The wrinkled face of Rue, the ghost of Heceta Head, staring from an attic window, has frightened away workers in the past.

of a lighthouse keeper whose baby died and was buried in the front yard (one old photo of the house does show what appears to be a small gravestone). The most well known encounter with Rue happened to a contractor working in the attic of the house. The contractor, Jim, was working by one of the windows when he saw the image of someone standing behind him reflected in the glass. He turned around to see who was in the small space with him when he was confronted by a very old, and very wrinkled lady dressed in old-fashioned pioneer clothes. She was completely three-dimensional, but as she moved towards him, Jim noticed, to his shock, that she was gliding instead of walking — indeed, her dressed stopped half a foot above the floor and there weren't any feet to be seen. As she glided closer and closer, he realized that there was no way to avoid her unless he ran right through her, and in his panic, that's exactly what he did, diving through the access panel leading to the attic and dropping over ten feet to the floor. Without breaking stride or even pausing for breath, in the blink of an eye he was in his truck and racing away. Being something of an artist, after he calmed down he drew a picture of the ghostly apparition as soon as he arrived home, but it strangely disappeared before he could show it to anyone.

A few days later, after some coaxing, he reluctantly returned to the house to paint around some windows that had been broken in the attic. He felt slightly braver this time since he was outside the house. However, as he stared through the opening where the windows had been, there was Rue, staring back at him. This time he decided twice was enough and he walked off the job for good. He called the caretakers a few days later to mention that he had left a pile of broken glass in the attic, and that same night the caretakers heard a noise in the attic, a sound like someone sweeping up broken glass with a wooden broom. The next day, they went to the attic and found that all the glass had been swept into small neat piles. By Rue.

Gold Hill

Near the town of Gold Hill is a roughly circular area known as the Oregon Vortex. This area of unusual geomagnetic energy was well known to the local natives, whose horses refused to enter the area, and so did they, declaring the area forbidden ground.

According to a local scientist, the vortex is a large, spherical pool of energy, half of it above ground and half below, affecting an area about 165 feet in diameter. It appears to cause a number of strange effects, much like crop circles do in England. Supposedly, aircraft flying high above the vortex are also affected by the energy. The scientist apparently burned most of his notes after conducting experiments at the site, famously claiming, "The world is not ready for this!"

The Oregon Vortex is a highly localized area where the normal laws of physics do not work.

Rock Point Cemetery is located close to the Vortex. Maybe that's why weird phenomena has been witnessed there, like a hooded ghost and even flames shooting out of a crypt.

For instance, in the old Assay cabin, balls appear to roll upwards, brooms can be made to stand by themselves, and outside, visitors seem to change height. Some of these are obviously the result of the extremely odd angles of the background buildings. But others, who knows? Maybe John Lister, the Scottish scientist who first discovered the area, knows. His ghost has been seen resting against the wall of the old log cabin, laughing and having a great time. Naturally, skeptics are keen to insist that most of the effects are the results of optical illusions, although many people have reported feeling very dizzy after a spell inside the whirlpool of energy.

In the local graveyard, Rock Point Cemetery, stories have been told of a ghost that wanders through the silent stones, wearing a dark hooded cloak and carrying a lantern. He's not the only one, either, as tales of weird lights, sounds, and even leaps of flame from crypts have been witnessed. It's assumed that this particular graveyard is extra active because of the spillover effects from the Vortex close by.

Chapter Six

Jousting Spirits

Jacksonville

The former inhabitants of this town had a number of hard luck stories that resulted in ghostly activity that just won't quit. For instance, in the 1850s Herbert Helms and his wife started a saloon in the town. In the Helms family, the youngest child died of smallpox during the winter. The ground was so frozen that the little body was buried in the front of the house. By the 1870s, the family had built a bigger house, probably right on top of the grave. Then another tragedy struck when two of their daughters died of typhoid in one week. As if that wasn't enough hardship, later another daughter was murdered by her estranged husband. Since that time the spirit of an old lady can be seen wandering the halls, and the ghost of a little girl sits and cries at the bottom of the stairs.

In another house, the ghost of a gambler who was either murdered or committed suicide haunts the place by opening and closing doors, walking noisily around, and on one occasion, casually sitting on the edge of a bed.

Yet another building, eerily called the Storm House, was well known locally to be thoroughly and completely haunted. In the 1930s a family was offered the home as a place to stay, rent-free. One family jumped at the deal that they knew wouldn't last long. Of course, the neighbors knew that they wouldn't last long in the home, either. They knew of the reputation of the house, and that the original owners, who were bootleggers, had killed a man and also put in numerous trapdoors. Soon enough, the new family found the secret trapdoors and also a bloodstained staircase. Heavy footsteps were often heard going from the stairway to a trapdoor. Each day at 3 o'clock, whoever was in the room would suddenly feel compelled to stare at the trapdoor. The only actual ghost to be seen was that of a barefoot woman in a black cape. Soon, the family had had enough and left; afterwards, the entire house mysteriously burned to the ground.

Another house in town, called the Old Hall, features a Green Lady ghost that you definitely don't want to encounter. It's not that she's all that scary, but rumor has it that you'll *die* sometime in the two weeks after meeting her.

Klamath Falls

This town, located in southern Oregon and close to northern California is home to its fair share of spooks, all in public buildings, like the Old Hospital, thought to be the first hospital in Oregon. It used to be a place where visitors could rent rooms. However, the fact that it was full of apparitions that could be seen wandering around (especially by children), made it less than an attractive place to spend an evening.

The Linkville Cemetery, at over 150 years old, has seen plenty of burials, so it's no wonder that there are many reports of strange noises in the area. One grave in particular is rumored to glow bright green on every full moon.

Even the local Mazama High School football field is haunted. The field itself sits rather high off the ground, leading to the legend that it was erected over a graveyard. That is also the reason why scary cries and mournful noises can be heard from under the bleachers if the town loses a game. Talk about pressure to perform!

However, the most frightening building is the old Oregon Institute of Technology building, which has a reputation as a haunt of Dominican monks. From various wide-eyed reports, witnesses have heard victims screaming as they're being skinned alive and the cries of animals being mutilated. Dominican ghosts have been seen...in addition to the blood that stains the outside of the building. According to local rumors the place is also used for frightening occult practices during the full moon.

Lincoln City

This town on the Oregon coast even has spooks in its Visitor's Bureau. One of the ladies who work there has encountered a presence in the building and can feel the ghost lounging around. The local fire station keeps a number of vintage fire trucks, and in one of them the presence of a ghost named Bob can be felt riding shotgun. Firefighters say that he often accompanies them on calls.

Just outside of town lies a stretch of highway called the Van Duzer Corridor that is presented to tourists as a scenic highway, but is felt by others to be Oregon's own Area 51. Strange lights have been seen to hover in the sky and mysterious people appear and disappear on the road. Some people who have driven on the twisting highway have felt that their vehicle wasn't under their control while others have reported what might be a secret military base lurking in the deep woods. They say that a forest road was closed by the government in the 1970s, giving rise to the secret base theory. There definitely is a government-testing site close by that is closed to the public.

At one time a police officer, Dale, was responsible for investigating all the strange and unusual happenings in this area—including when there were signs of satanic activity in the area known as Devil's Lake. These weren't the usual high school knocking-over-gravestones signs, but real occult work involving animal sacrifices, so it was necessary for Dale to find the culprits before things got out of hand. It was decided to raid the scene of the biggest annual event, which occurred on Halloween, by boat in the early evening. The day was completely normal, but as evening neared, a wind suddenly whipped up out of nowhere, causing white-capped waves to crash about in the lake. It would be impossible to take the boat out in those conditions and the big raid had to be postponed. Had the coven arranged for the weather to hide their nefarious rites?

Ghostly happenings are so much a part of the local landscape that the Chamber of Commerce has announced an "eeek-o-tour" that will take visitors to all the area haunts.

Ghosts, Spirits, and Legends in the Lincoln City Area

It seems that spirits like living in and around Lincoln City as much as live humans do—perhaps because of the rich coastal history, a variety of Native American sacred places, or simply the intense emotion of sea tragedies and storms. If you enjoy seeking out phantoms, you can take your own Eeeeeeko Tour. This tour can be self-guided, or with advance notice the Lincoln City Visitor and Convention Bureau may be able to arrange step-on service. Call 800-452-2151 to arrange that service or for more information.

Breakfast with "Matilda"

The Wildflower Grill at 4250 Northeast Highway 101 has its own resident benevolent spirit, a woman they call Matilda. Although Matilda most frequently makes her presence known by opening and closing cabinets, she has made other, more personal contacts as well.

The Wildflower Grill has a resident ghost named Matilda who has been seen by guests and staff.

On one occasion she rattled the locked doorknob of the employee restroom. When she didn't get a response as immediate as she wished for, Matilda simply pushed the door open—without unlocking it. But she refused to make herself visible to the occupant. One of the owners has, however, seen Matilda, who walked past him in the restaurant and simply disappeared on its balcony. Maybe Matilda stays because the breakfasts at Wildflower are unbeatable. This is a great place to start your day and your tour off right!

Pioneer Cemetery

Many folks have felt the presence of spirits at Pioneer Cemetery. It is on the inland side of South Highway 101, just across the road from the Inn at Spanish Head, in the 4000 block. Even if you don't feel the presence, the view is stunning and the gravestones interesting.

North Lincoln County Historical Museum

More than one spirit frequents the North Lincoln County Historical Museum at 4907 Southwest Highway 101. The former curator frequently heard "human" noises traveling about from room to room and felt the benevolent presence of someone, even though no other humans were in the building. Psychics have felt the presence of a group that occasionally meets around the conference room table on the second floor.

For those who love history or just "old stuff," the North Lincoln County Historical Museum is a real treat. The downstairs exhibit gallery includes: displays on Native American history with examples of baskets and beadwork; early settlement and homesteading displays that show early tools and household items; and dairy, fishing, and cannery displays with artifacts from those industries. The upstairs gallery focuses on tourism, celebrating the age of the automobile with information on the first cars and roads to the area. Roadside attractions, early tourism promotions like the notorious "Redhead Roundup," and one-of-a-kind businesses like the Pixie Kitchen are also exhibited. A hands-on children's corner will keep younger children entertained while their parents tour the museum.

Siletz Bay Schooner

Some 150 years ago a sailing vessel washed up in Siletz Bay at the south end of Lincoln City, just two blocks south of the Museum on Southwest 51st Street. Seen as recently as ten years ago, the vessel, likely a schooner or a brig, has been buried in the mudflats of the bay, which was a working harbor in the early part of last century. That vessel may be the source of a ghost ship, which has occasionally been seen sailing into the bay, though not on the water, and then vanishing into thin air. The phantom ship was seen as recently as 2001 by a bay area resident as it sped full-sail toward her living room window. Siletz Bay is a good place to view wildlife, stroll on the beach, and take photographs.

Spouting Horn in Depoe Bay

A more restless ghost spends his time near the bar in the Spouting Horn Restaurant in Depoe Bay, just eight miles south of Lincoln City. His appearances were so frequent that children of the owners and employees finally dubbed him Ralph to give him a more familiar identity. In the mid-eighties he appeared in a cook's apron, arms crossed, and staring as if to suggest the humans he encountered were intruding on his territory. He frequently crosses the hallway to the dining room or streaks across the restaurant when only owners or employees are present. Have afternoon dessert and chat with the staff about Ralph. You'll need to pay for your dessert, but not for a sighting of Ralph.

Ghosts "Not Open to the Public"

A few haunted sites in Lincoln City cannot be visited by the general public. In a private home in the Roads End area, a young girl, seen only from the waist down, occasionally cooks breakfast for her father. Jealous of the current owners' grandchildren, the girl regularly turns the children's pictures to face the wall. She is believed to be the daughter of a man who worked in the area until the early hours of the morning and later shot himself while standing at the edge of Cascade Head.

Devils Lake Fire Station in north Lincoln City houses the spirit of a former volunteer firefighter who makes as his home the first fire truck put into service at the station that is kept in the back bay. The bay area is always cold, even when the weather is hot and the doors are closed. A few of the volunteers have heard him walking up and down the stairs during the night, and one of the volunteers found him napping on the break room couch. But he vanished in an instant. Some of today's volunteers believe that "Bob" still rides along with them to fires.

Although these apparitions may not be sought directly, the stories about them have been captured on film. To get the full experience of their tales watch the "Oregon Ghost Explorer." A copy may be obtained from the Visitor and Convention Bureau. Call 800-452-2151 or 541-996-1274.

The Legend of Devils Lake

Spirit? Monster? Devil? No one knows for sure. But as legend has it, a long-tentacled creature inhabits the 680-acre fresh water lake on the northeast side of Lincoln City.

Chapter Six: Jousting Spirits

The lake, formed by sand dunes and beach deposits that blocked the lower end of the valley 14,000 years ago, empties into the ocean through the D River, at 120 feet long, recorded as the shortest river in the world. Centuries ago, when it was known as Indian Bay, many Siletz Indians vanished into its waters when they were pulled from their vessels by giant tentacles. On one particular occasion, so the legend goes, a Chief sent warriors across the waters in an effort to win a maiden from the warrior of her choice. The waters boiled, and giant tentacles wrapped around the warriors and pulled them from their canoes. In an effort to pacify the devil, feasts were regularly held on the shores of the lake and sacrifices were offered to the Lake Devil, whose hideous head rose high above the surface.

Something huge and tentacled has pulled natives from their boats in the past at Devil's Lake, and the thing lurks there still.

Chapter Seven

Mysterious Manifestations

Medford

One of the earliest reports of ghostly activity was mentioned in a newspaper account in 1911. According to the story, locals in east Medford were aware of a ghost that took form at 3 a.m. each night except Sunday (it must have been a religious ghost). It would then cross Bear Creek Bridge, plowing its way through anything and everything. Far from being scared, the residents were quite proud of their apparition.

Ghosts don't have to worry about being arrested, so they have had no problem in haunting the Justice Building located downtown. Strange things occurred on the fourth floor, and always after 1 o'clock in the morning. Cleaners who worked alone in the big empty building would suddenly find themselves in the dark as the lights shut off, after which a disembodied voice would call their name. Even the most hardened janitors would have chills running down their spines.

Monmouth

Western Oregon College boasts a nice theatre, so nice, in fact, that the first theatre instructor still roams the building. Many students have heard the echoing footsteps of George Harding as he walks across the stage.

Mount Angel

At Providence Benedictine Nursing Center, ghosts of past residents can be felt or seen sitting in chairs, looking out windows, and in general frequenting the last building they were in.

Some people have also seen a nun walking the halls, and often others have felt a tap on their shoulder and heard someone ask, "Can you help me?"...only to turn around and find no one there.

Mount Hood

Rhododendron Village is a heritage site built on the area of an original logging camp near Mount Hood. The Village was a place where visitors could come and stay and enjoy the mountain surroundings, but they often didn't get much sleep, since the place is still active with the comings and goings of its former inhabitants. Doors open and slam shut, lights turn on and off, and heavy footsteps can be heard walking across the floor at night. The ghosts have even been caught on camera...like the time an old organ was photographed and the face of a woman in period clothes could be seen in the reflection of a mirror hanging above the instrument. The area was a burial ground for both settlers and Native Americans, and as a result, all the buildings, even the new ones built to replace original ones, are haunted. As usual, whenever an older building is renovated, it stirs up the ghostly pot and paranormal activity would boil over for some time.

Chapter Eight

No Peace for Ghosts

Nehalem

Usually ghosts are found by owners of homes or in other buildings frequented by lots of people. Sometimes though, spirits are attracted to spirits of the drinking kind, as in the case of Nehalem Winery. The building has had its share of strange happenings for many years, but recently a ghost-hunting team called C.A.S.P.E.R. (Central Arizona Specialists in Paranormal Events Research) performed an investigation of their own at the site, where they were able to get an electronic voice phenomenon, or EVP (see glossary), of a woman's voice on tape. Members of the team heard voices, saw moving shadows, and felt a presence. In one bedroom, investigators saw a shadow slink out of a closet and across the room where it formed into the image of a man.

Apparently, passing away doesn't always mean blissful peace, since the team heard voices arguing in an upstairs room, with a woman's voice groaning "kill me, kill me" caught on tape.

Newport Lighthouse

It seems that most lighthouses are haunted. Newport Lighthouse, first lit in 1884, is the second oldest in the state, and comes complete with a ghost story that starts over a hundred years ago, when, in the middle of winter in raging seas, a sloop entered the bay. The crew of the vessel spoke a strange foreign language, and the captain was a wild looking man with an ugly scar down his face. However, the passengers consisted of a well-respected man called Trevenard and his daughter Zina. After the vessel took on fresh water, Trevenard asked if his daughter could stay in the town until his return in a couple of weeks, and so she went to stay in the Yaquina Bay Hotel.

Weeks turned into months, and after a year the ship still hadn't returned, but Zina was happy with the many new friends she had made. In December of 1884 she and some friends decided to visit the old lighthouse for fun. They were given a key by the landlady who warned them to leave *before* nightfall—a time when many frightening sounds had been heard coming from the old structure.

They spent the day exploring the place, and on the second floor found an area where an iron door had been hidden behind some paneling. After prying the door open, they discovered a small room about eight feet deep that ended in a sudden drop all the way to the ocean far below. The kids noticed a sudden turn in the weather as rain pelted the building and the wind whipped the sea. The group took little time in getting ready to leave. One young man was sent to lock the front door and found Zina waiting there. She had left her hankerchief inside and had to retrieve it, and told the man not to wait for her, but just to lock the door after she entered, and that she would leave by the kitchen door. The

Newport Lighthouse was the site of the strange disappearance of Zina, and the haunt of the spirit of a sea captain.

A hitchhiker encountered a ghostly couple at the lighthouse that psychically knew of his personal troubles.

man did wait rather anxiously for a while, but after a short time without sight of her he assumed she must have passed him in the fog and so he rejoined the group farther down the path.

When he reached the group, he was surprised to see that she wasn't among them. As a murmur of concern fell over the teenagers, a blood-curdling scream split the air, and the group ran back to the lighthouse, hearing more chilling screams as they got nearer. They burst inside the building and on the second floor found Zina's bloodstained hankerchief, but no sign of the girl. The iron door had been replaced and couldn't be moved. Although a massive search was undertaken, nobody ever saw poor Zina again. The blood on the floor is still visible to this day.

One of the ghosts that make the lighthouse his home is that of the whaling ship captain Evan McClure. He can be seen there still, complete with a sailor's wild red hair and full beard. According to legend, there are two things he needs in order to finally rest — a place to stay and a companion to join him. Any takers?

No more than twenty years ago, a hitchhiker camped out in the front yard of the lighthouse. In the middle of the night, he noticed the lights were on inside the building. Then the door opened and a woman in a long white dress appeared in the doorway, along with a huge man. There was a soft glow surrounding her as she walked over to the hitchhiker, who was now feeling guilty for having been found camping on their land. She said to him, "Don't worry, Harold. You're welcome here." He tried to explain that his name wasn't Harold. She softly told him he would find a job soon, and then returned to the lighthouse. During that night, a tugboat and a light aircraft both reported seeing the lights of the lighthouse blazing. And the hitchhiker did find employment shortly after the encounter.

The Oar House is a pleasant Bed & Breakfast built from wood gathered from shipwrecks. It started out as a boarding house. In a town full of dockworkers and sailors, it was probably inevitable that in time it became a bordello. According to legend, a young girl stayed there while waiting for her boyfriend to return from the sea, and when it became obvious that he wasn't coming back, she threw herself from the third-story window. She still frequents the house, even lying down in bed beside a former owner.

Neahkahnie Bay

Neahkahnie Mountain is the location of a fabled fortune in pirate gold. Although many have tried, the treasure, guarded by spirits, has never been found.

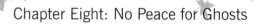

Neahkahnie Mountain Treasure

The local Native Americans tell how, long ago, a pair of sailing ships were fighting each other in the bay. After a barrage of canon fire, one of the ships was driven onto the reefs. At low tide, the men from the ship, all white except for one black man who was much larger than the rest, came ashore, dragging a chest that was so heavy it took several men to move it. They dug a pit on the nearby mountain and carefully lowered the chest into it. They then killed the black man and threw his body on top of it, to guard the contents, and then filled in the pit.

The whites stayed in the area for a couple of years, but by that time the Indians had had enough of their boorish manners, violent tendencies, and their habit of taking Native women whenever they wished. They had definitely outstayed their welcome and a confederation of Clatsop, Tillamook, and Nehalem Indians attacked the camp, killing all the inhabitants. They buried the bodies in a mass grave near where the treasure was buried. Afraid of the evil black spirit, they never attempted to dig up the treasure chest, and never talked about the burials either. As far as anyone knows, the treasure is still there. There are mysterious markings carved in the rocks, and skeletons and remains of a ship have been found at nearby Three Rocks Beach in northern Lincoln County. Many people have searched in vain for the cursed treasure, including at least five people who died in the attempt.

Oregon City

Situated adjacent to Portland, Oregon City was laid out in 1840 by the flamboyant John McLoughlin, a doctor who

The tall form of John McLoughlin, one of the area's original movers and shakers, has been seen ducking through doorways in his home.

had traveled west and landed a position with the Hudson Bay Company.

The doctor, towering over the average man, had a steely gaze, long flowing white hair, and a quick temper to boot. His spirit can still be seen wandering through his old house (now a museum) on Center Street. His shadow can be glimpsed as it ducks through doorways, footsteps are heard, and on occasion his favorite chair, a rocker, creaks back and forth by itself. In addition, some people have claimed to see a woman standing in an upstairs window as they walk by on the street below. Could this be the shade of McLoughlin's Cree Indian wife?

The house next door to McLoughlin is also haunted, by a young boy and an older man.

As if that wasn't enough, the house right next door is haunted as well. Built by Dr. Forbes Barclay, another Hudson's Bay man, one of the bedrooms is visited by the doctor's seaman brother, Uncle Sandy. This man often stayed here when his ship was in dock and even now he will sit in a chair and stare at anyone using his bed…before disappearing back through a wall. Well, maybe he was tired and wanted the bed for himself. He's not the only spirit roaming the house, because a young redheaded boy has been seen running and playing in the hallway.

Chapter Nine

Portland's Paranormal

The city of Portland was still under a thousand hardy souls in the early 1850s, and only started to really hustle and bustle after the Civil War, when it's location on the Columbia River made it the perfect spot for shipping lumber and fish, along with other produce, to the rest of the West Coast and abroad. In the winter the roads were deep troughs of mud, with hundreds of stumps of fallen trees a constant hazard. In fact, the city was (and still is) called Stumptown by many. By the late 1800s, it had become the largest metropolis in the Northwest.

Millions of people came to Portland to visit the Lewis and Clark Exposition in the early 1900s and thousands stayed, working at the many mills, warehouses, and lumberyards that dotted the city. Streetcar routes connected the profusion of different neighborhoods, pulling all the outlying areas into one large urban space called Portland.

The city boasts of having both the largest park in the country (Forest Park) as well as the smallest, the twenty-four-inch park at a road intersection. It's also home to Nike, Addidas, Intel, and other large companies, and is known as a hotbed for the graphic arts and advertising professions.

As a melting pot for various nationalities and personalities, from the seamy dockside trades to the airy refines of mansions, it's no wonder that Portland is home to more ghosts than any other city in the state, starting with its university.

Started as a Catholic school in 1901, Portland University is over one hundred years old. The campus, located with a great view over Willamette River, is home to more than just students, as Christie Hall — one of the oldest buildings — has a reputation for having a haunted basement; the basement was where the dying priests spent their last days. Students have reported curtains moving and the unmistakable feeling of being watched there.

As has already been mentioned, doing repairs on a building is a good way to stir up the spirits. Workers made so much noise while making repairs on the oldest building, Waldschmidt Hall, that the resident ghost *upped roots* and *moved* into an entirely different building, Kenna Hall! This spirit is a boy who drowned in the nearby river in the 1800s, and was seen by at least one person, standing in a hallway, hair and clothes soaking wet, staring at the student.

The Commons building, where the commissary is located, is home to a cranky poltergeist that chases employees with pushcarts that move on their own, throws pots and pans, shakes pictures, and generally makes a nuisance of itself.

Another seat of higher learning, the Lewis and Clark College, has it's own paranormal claim to fame. According to legend, if a person goes to the center of the campus in the wee hours of the night, the sound of an angry mob, complete with yelling and screaming, can be heard. Furthermore, at least once or twice a witness has reportedly seen a number of spirits being *chased* by even *more* spirits!

Ghosts of little kids are always creepy, and the ones trapped inside this carousel are no different.

On a large island in the middle of the Columbia River, there is a large mall in the space where Jantzen Beach, Portland's answer to Coney Island, used to be. The original Jantzen Beach had it all — fairground rides, entertainment, and a very big and very fast merry-go-round. The old fairground is just a memory now, but the merry-go-round is still a star attraction in the mall. Some of the kids riding the colorful horses never seem to want to leave, and apparently, two youngsters never have.

There is a small building in the center of the ride, and when the door is open some people have seen two young children playing inside, a boy and a girl. They look out on the children riding the painted ponies and telepathically encourage them to come inside and play. Of course, the creepy captive kids never get any takers!

🐾 🐾 🐾 🐾 🐾

Usually living in apartment buildings can be noisy. The North Denver Street apartments also have noise and the feeling of being watched by unseen eyes.

You're alone in the North Denver Street Apartments. The old stone building was once, allegedly, a brothel, but now contains a number of housing units. Being over one hundred years old, there is enough psychic residue in the place to create an atmosphere filled with disembodied voices, footsteps, windows opening themselves, and the ever-present feeling of being watched.

What is it about old apartment buildings that is so attractive to the spirit world? Another building, the Falcon Apartments, harbors at least two ghosts, known by name. Both men, while alive, enjoyed sitting in the chairs in the hallway—and both can be seen in the same place now. Jimmy is still in his seat (although it is no longer there), while poor Mr. Cooke has to stand. Other manifestations include banging on the mailboxes and something that knocks on all of the doors on one side of the building.

And what about the Granada Court Apartments? There are unseen eyes watching the tenants there, and possibly the ghost of a young child. Maybe even the spirit of a woman who had been killed nearby many years ago. In any case, it can be hard to get some shut-eye in the building!

A woman who managed an apartment building in the Portland area had a strange encounter with a person who was *not* of this world. Having worked in her profession for over twenty years, she thought she had seen it all. Many types of people come looking for apartments; some nice, some not so nice. However, one day a young man about eighteen years old came to ask about a room. One look at his eyes caused the woman to shudder and a very real feeling of dread overwhelmed her. His eyes were completely back, no difference between the iris and the pupil. She felt that it would be the end of her if she let him in and so she slammed the door in his face.

Others have felt the same way when they meet the Black-eyed People, as they are known. They all tell the same story of dread...a feeling of being the prey to some unspeakable predatory creature. It's even creepier when the "beings" are children. One witness recalled hearing a slow, mechanical knocking on her door, and when she looked out the window she saw two children with completely black eyes. One demanded, "Let us in." The woman refused and got as far away as possible from the pair.

🍂 🍂 🍂 🍂 🍂

The North Portland Library has ghosts both inside and outside the building. The lovely red-brick building features a second floor meeting room that is locked unless a function is taking place. Security cameras also monitor the room, and it's these cameras that caught the image of a man sitting in a chair in the empty room. When employees investigated, the room was empty. In fact, while one employee watched the man on the monitor, another employee would enter the room just as

People walking at night in the street outside the North Portland Library have reported hearing heavy footsteps trailing them. There is another ghost inside the building.

the ghost disappeared. This has happened so often that it's taken for granted now.

Ominous heavy footsteps trail the unwary that walk on the sidewalk outside the library late at night. On many occasions, footsteps can be heard walking right up to the unsuspecting pedestrian, who then whips around to see who it is—only to find thin air. There is a mortuary close by. Could the souls of the newly departed be walking the area aimlessly in the middle of the night?

🍁 🍁 🍁 🍁 🍁

Of course, there are many private homes in the Portland area that have their own resident spirits.

🍃 One house on Bank Street was the haunt of a number of ghosts wearing plaid, or possibly even kilts!

🍃 A Mohawk Street house had an apparition of the white, misty kind—it could also be heard walking around and even yelling "Hey you!" every now and then. Apparently his name was Carlos, although how that was known isn't known itself.

🍃 On Watts Street sits a house that was the location of a murder/suicide in the 1970s. After that tragic event, the home was the focus for much paranormal activity, including visions of a man standing in the driveway and a lady who will stand and watch you. Neither ghost has a lot to say and the people living in the house found that the pair makes for interesting companions.

However, that cannot be said of an evil entity that was encountered at a house off of Sandy Boulevard. About thirty years ago, a young girl living in the house was home alone, and heard talking and commotion from the locked attic. Of course, this was pretty scary, but then she saw movement in the basement and saw eyes peeking up at her from the bottom of the stairs. Frightened, she ran out of the house and across the street to the neighbors, but since it was a weekday, they weren't in (which is why her parents weren't home either). As she looked back at her house, she was horrified to see a ghost, complete with dark red eyes and pointed teeth, staring at her. When her parents finally drove up, she begged them not to go into the house, but they did anyway. They didn't see any ghosts, but the behavior of the father became increasingly violent until they moved away.

❧ On a cheerier note, a home on Princeton Street was being haunted, *or looked after*, depending on your view, by the wife of the original owner. The wife had died, but when the husband was away on business, she still came by to tuck her daughter into bed each night. The widower eventually moved, but the woman stayed with the house, rocking back and forth in a chair that could be seen going by itself without anyone sitting in it.

❧ A house in southeast Portland was the location of numerous sightings of a man who would stand at the foot of the bed in the bedroom and stare at the person sleeping. Once he was seen outside the house looking in on a woman who was feeling particularly uneasy at the same moment. A neighbor in the area said it was the spirit of a man who had committed suicide in the house thirty years previously.

❧ ❧ ❧ ❧ ❧

Some of the hauntings in Portland occur in public buildings, so ghost-hunters may have a chance to get lucky.

❧ The Crystal Ballroom, a live music venue on Burnside Road, was originally opened as a dancehall back in the Roaring Twenties. It even featured a floating dance floor that swayed slightly with the dancers, and the shiny wooden floor echoed to the sound of hundreds of pairs of jitterbugging feet. More recently, it has reopened for live music concerts and many great bands have performed on its stage. Even when the place is closed, managers have heard groups of people talking and laughing in the building, or heard the unmistakable sound of footsteps on the hardwood floor. One manager even got a glimpse of what looked like an actual person casually walking by, but who wasn't anywhere to be found seconds later.

🌿 The White Eagle Tavern is easily the most famous haunted bar in Portland. The one hundred-year-old establishment started out as a rough bar (having the nickname of "The Bucket of

The White Eagle Tavern is filled with ghosts of unlucky prostitutes, but is still a very cool place to visit.

Blood" at the time because of the frequent fights that went on there), and before too long it became better known as a brothel, and a pretty seedy one, too. Having said that, it's also been home to a great many bands, including ZZ Top, Robert Cray, and a host of others. In fact, there is live music there every night of the week.

The place is also filled with paranormal activity, including old coins mysteriously appearing, invisible hands groping the customers, and even a phantom presence that leaves the bar, walks over to the bathroom, and flushes the toilet. Located close to the Columbia River, it was said that the basement rooms were reserved for black and Chinese prostitutes, who were treated very poorly. They were rarely allowed to leave the rooms, and if they got pregnant and had children the offspring were quickly disposed of, as were the prostitutes themselves when they grew too old to satisfy the customers.

The upstairs rooms were for the white working ladies, and it was here that one particular lady named Rose was killed in a fit of passion by one of her regulars. He had fallen in love with her and begged her to leave the brothel with him, but she refused, afraid of the rough man who ran the establishment. Finally, her suitor stabbed and killed her in a fit of rage, and since then her sad spirit lingers on. Many patrons and employees have heard her plaintive wailing and sobbing.Another spirit is Sam, an orphan who was a lifelong kitchen helper with a big alcohol problem. Both of these characters still haunt the rooms above the bar, which were closed off to the public for many years because of the eerie goings-on. The basement is even worse, with mysterious sounds emanating beneath the floor, a dark and depressing atmosphere, and the apparition of Old Barney who hangs around.

The Lotus has an unspeakable horror hiding in the basement.

🍂 Another drinking establishment, the Lotus Nightclub, located downtown, has an extremely creepy and evil presence in the basement, so much so that employees can't even bring themselves to talk about it. One bartender, after cleaning up for the night and putting away all the glasses, went to the cursed basement and heard the CO_2 canister being activated, which can only be done when it is being used. After hurrying back upstairs, he noticed an upside-down shotglass on the bar that certainly wasn't there before.

🍂 Another place, Joe's Cellar in northwest Portland, is also chock full of ghosts, ranging from a prostitute to a man who died in a fire, and even includes a spirit weiner dog! EVPs have been recorded in the building that, like most structures close to the docks, was once a brothel.

The Benson Hotel downtown is so elegant that even its ghost is impeccably dressed.

🍂 The Benson Hotel in downtown Portland on Broadway was built in 1921 and was meant to be the West Coast's answer to the European-style hotels on the East Coast. This meant Italian marble floor, rich walnut paneling, and chandeliers — the whole hog. Some of the ritzy guests still make an appearance, like the gentleman dressed in a smart black coat who walks regally down the staircase, disappearing just as he reaches the lobby, and the lady in white who has been seen walking the hallways in the upper stories.

Another luxury hotel, also on Broadway, is the elegant Heathman Hotel, and it too is haunted by ghostly footsteps, strange whispers in the hallways, items being moved about in the rooms, and the usual cold spots. Apparently, a girl had committed suicide by jumping out of a tenth-floor window at some time in the past, and now every room ending in "03" (903, 303, etc.) is haunted by her spirit as she plummeted to her death.

Another fine hotel is the Heathman, that apparently has haunted rooms that correspond to the path taken by a suicide who jumped from a tenth floor window.

Cathedral Park was the location of a rape and murder during the Forties, and the victim's screams can still be heard.

🍂 The Bagdad Theatre on Hawthorne was one of many pseudo-Arabian themed theatres built during the Art Deco period. The building seems to have peeping Tom type ghosts, because the kitchen help feel as if they're being watched through the swinging doors and patrons using the downstairs bathroom also feel eyes peering into them.

🍂 At one end of St. John's Bridge in north Portland is a lovely spot named Cathedral Park, in honor of the cathedral-like massive supports of the bridge that rise hundreds of feet in the air. In the 1940s, however, the area wasn't so gentrified, and a horrible crime was committed there. A fifteen-year-old high school student named Thelma was kidnapped here, held prisoner by a rapist for a week, and finally killed (her rapist was eventually caught and executed). On summer nights, terrified screams can still be heard echoing in the area. Police have been called to the site so often that they know exactly who is doing the screaming... and she is beyond help.

🍁 Pittock Mansion overlooks the greater Portland area, and was the grand summerhouse of industrialist Henry Pittock and his wife Georgiana. Heavy boots can be heard walking in the vicinity and might be those of the gardener. Unseen hands often move a portrait of Henry, and a guest once saw the form of an older lady reflected in the glass of a painting. The heady smell of Georgiana's favorite roses can often be detected throughout the home.

The heavy footsteps of a former gardener have been heard on the grounds of the Pittock Mansion.

The Columbian Cemetery is located in about the noisiest part of Portland. Maybe that's why the spirits are restless.

You'd expect cemeteries to be haunted, and at least one is. The Columbian Cemetery, now located in a very industrial area, could hardly be called a peaceful area for eternal rest. Graffiti covers the walls that hem in one side of the area and a never-ending stream of semis, dump trucks, and tractor-trailers rumble by a few feet from the entrance. Even so, many people there have seen the ghostly form of a lady called Lydia.

The Old Town Pizza Company, located close to Chinatown, has its very own celebrity ghost. The spirit, Nina, not only has a brick with her name inscribed on it, but also a portrait hanging in the restaurant. She can be seen as a white-colored ghost (or a lady in a black dress, depending on who you talk to) who was apparently a victim of the city's notorious Shanghai Tunnels

The ghost of Nina comes with the meals at the Old Town Pizza Company.

that start very near to the eatery. The Tunnels make their way underground through sections of the city, and it was in these tunnels that men were often beaten senseless. Upon awakening they would, with dismay, find themselves far out to sea on a ship, pressed into service, or shanghaied. In addition to men, women — like Nina — would be kidnapped, taken to the Tunnels, and sold into the thriving sex industry, often ending up overseas. Nina had decided to spill the beans on the unsavory business to missionaries, but unsurprisingly was found dead after having been thrown down an elevator shaft. She can still sometimes be seen on the balcony, or a soft hint of her perfume can be detected.

Edgefield Winery in nearby Tigard was once a poor farm and then a nursing home. Much psychic activity has been reported above the wine cellars in the area that used to be the morgue.

Chapter Ten

Roaming Spirits...& Other Supernatural Occurrences

Rogue River

There is a house in this area that features a haunted wooden mantelpiece that would start to make heavy creaking noises on the same night every year. Upon investigation, it turned out that the wood came from a beam that outlaws had used to hang a man before escaping long ago. The hanging occurred on the same day as the creaking sound is heard.

More recently, a couple moved into an old 1846 farmhouse that had been haunted long before they arrived. For instance, one of the daughters was talking on the phone when she heard the door open and someone walk inside, but the room was empty when she went to investigate. Another of the daughters heard movement all through the night and was unable to sleep. In a final example, the wife had been working outside in the heat with her husband and went inside to get some rest. While she was lying in bed, she felt her husband come in, lie down

94

beside her, and cuddle. When she awoke, she found he had silently left the room. However, when she asked her husband later why he left her alone, he replied, "I don't know who you've been sleeping with, but it certainly wasn't me. I've been outside all afternoon."

There was a place called the Old McAlder homestead that was lived in by (who else?) Old Man McAlder and his wife, an Indian who was the daughter of a medicine man and had some of his supernatural powers. However, even with those powers, you have to go sometime and, when she knew she was dying she told her husband that her spirit would ensure that the home would always be a happy one, with fresh bread in the oven, cool water to drink, and a nice fire in the fireplace. When she died, her husband only lasted another year before he, too, was gone.

Many years later, a surveyor in the area became lost during a rainstorm. When darkness fell, he couldn't believe his luck when he saw the cabin with its lights shining a welcome beacon. He stopped inside and even though no one was there, he found a warm fire going along with a loaf of fresh bread and a jug of fresh water. Soon he was fast asleep. The next morning he found the rest of his survey party and told them of the wonderful cabin. They didn't believe him for a minute and so he insisted on taking the group there. When they came to where he spent the night, though, all they found was an ancient shack that was falling to pieces and obviously hadn't been lived in for ages.

Another welcoming place was the Galesville Hotel. The hotel was popular back in the old days, but as time wore on it became less so. A family bought the place as a private residence sometime later. The owners reported that a phantom stagecoach used to rattle up the drive every day at precisely 11 a.m., and the voices of non-existent guests could clearly be heard talking outside. The building is gone now.

Salem

Salem, as Oregon's capitol, has good reason to hold the most ghost accounts. This probably has more to do with the fact that the town has been written about longer than any other for any special paranormal magnetic power than the area might hold.

The Salem area has been haunted long before settlers arrived. The local Native American Kalapuya tribe knew of a monster that frequented the mountains and valleys of Western Oregon. Its name was Chuchonnyhoof, and the goblin-like beast with an "iron hide" would lie in wait in the wild lands in order to capture and eat any unsuspecting people who ventured too far.

An early pioneer house from the year 1878 was long known to be haunted. The house, which had lain vacant for many years, included the usual trampling feet and shadowy figures among its ghostly happenings. This particular house also included a big, ghostly yellow dog that waited patiently in the street in front of the house.

In the Rosedale area of Salem is another haunted house from the same year. This old yellow house always had a strange and peculiar feel to it. One person who lived in the house for many years had reported to her parents as a young girl that she had seen a strange woman wandering around the yard. It was thought to be the spirit of a lady who had died in childbirth in the same house a number of years previously.

Fairview Hospital

The haunted place that's known far and wide in Oregon has to be that of the old asylum for the mentally handicapped, Fairview Hospital. Originally opened in 1904, the buildings and grounds have been the only home to thousands of unfortunate people over the years. Many were in different states of retardation or mental illness, but back in those early days, other people living outside of the norm, including vagrants, hitchhikers, and promiscuous girls were also sent here. Even those who weren't exhibiting signs of mental instability soon were in these surroundings. In addition, in early unenlightened days, they had very traumatic ways of dealing with the inmates, including forced sterilization,

Fairview Hospital, now overgrown, was the state mental asylum and as such was the location of many lobotomies, forced sterilizations and even deaths. No wonder it retains a very creepy feeling.

A virtual rabbit warren of underground tunnels connect the different buildings at Fairview. Notice the orb in this picture. *Courtesy of Luke and McKenzie Fountain*.

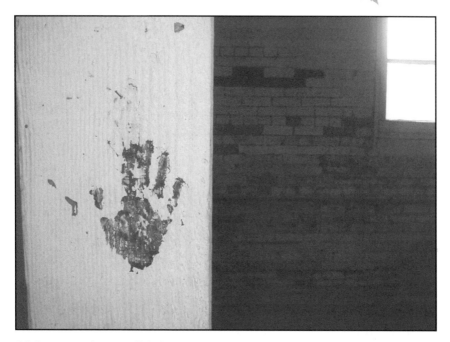

Of the many ghosts at Fairview, there includes an old woman, a young man who goes through lockers and a heavy psychic energy that can keep cars from starting. *Courtesy of Luke and McKenzie Fountain.*

lobotomies, and being strapped to beds or put in straightjackets. This treatment could be understandable given the large numbers of inmates and very small numbers of doctors and nurses to take care of them. Many didn't stay long. At least nine preventable deaths occurred at the hospital, and they weren't even counted among the two dozen bodies that had been buried on the grounds somewhere and then lost. Were they exhumed, or was a building erected over their final resting place? No one knows. What is known is that many spirits have been unable to leave this area, heavily laden with psychic tension.

Just two of the ghosts in the area include the form of an old woman who can be seen walking the grounds at night, especially near one of the school's cottages. Another ghost was often seen in the basement lounge of Holderness Cottage, one of the areas where some of the more aggressive inmates were kept. This spirit has been described as a man in his thirties who walks through the kitchen and lounge, casually going through the locked doors. He doesn't seem to notice the witness and goes about his business calmly.

One spooky occurrence happened while Fairview was open. A young patient had been in the middle of a bad epileptic seizure while on his own. A person ran to tell the staff that he needed immediate help, and they were able to calm the terrified child until he was well enough. It was only then that someone realized that the person who had warned them was the boy's mother, who had been dead for a number of years.

Other residents weren't as lucky as him. In 1923, one of the patients, Hollie Pollack, was discovered to be missing, and at the time it was assumed he had escaped the hospital grounds. However, a few weeks later bits of hair and skin were found in the hospital's water pipes and subsequently, his body was found drowned in the well. The area around the boarded up cistern is very haunted. Even now, workers who have made the mistake of parking their cars near the well find them unable to start later. Once the vehicles have been towed away, they restart with ease. Some have returned to park in the same area, only to find the same thing happen all over again.

Many of the buildings at Fairview are connected through a rabbit warren of tunnels. These obviously claustrophobic networks have been explored recently and contain unmistakable energies, as well as disembodied voices and footsteps, strange shadows, glowing orbs, and many other eerie phenomena.

🍂 🍂 🍂 🍂 🍂

Different sections in the Salem district have their own loyal ghosts. They include:

The Chemeketa-Court Historic District

This area contains a splendid collection of houses dating back to the 1870s. They include the old Bush House on Mission Street that is said to have spirits roaming within, although no one is positive if that is fact or legend. Apparently, during the early 1900s a young woman who suffered from schizophrenia lived in the house, and times being what they were, the family hid her in the basement, where she eventually died. She now haunts the house, and because of her life in the dark, cold cellar, now regularly likes to play with the thermostat. Another house nearby has a long history of hauntings that include candles mysteriously lighting themselves, windows opening and closing, objects moving of their own accord, nightmares terrorizing any young

A ghost who likes it very warm keeps turning up the thermostat at the Bush House.

person who stays there, and an evil energy that causes adults to inexplicably fight with each other. Understandably, the house has undergone a large succession of owners and is now an art gallery.

One area home features the familiar cold spot so often associated with ghosts, as well as the voice of a crying child and an angry male ghost who makes the hallway and back bedroom his home and refuses to leave. A final house in the neighborhood has a great example of the type of haunting that repeats like a videotape. Here, a Dutchman strangles his wife over and over in a crime that was first committed well over a hundred years ago.

Leslie Middle School in town is said to still be the home of the person it was named after — the late Mr. Leslie.

The Madrona area

This area of Salem only has one haunting, but it's a good one. The house was only built in the 1930s, but already harbors at least *seven* ghosts. In its troubled history, it has burnt to the ground twice, only to be rebuilt. Why all the activity? The house was built right over the worse place possible — an Indian burial ground. And, many of the people buried there were women who had been raped and killed by early settlers. One of the major ghosts in the house is a Native American warrior who guards it. No amount of encouragement has forced him to leave.

On a close par with the burial ground is the town's hanging grounds that were located on Lower Church Street next to Mill Creek. A couple of the large trees there have been the location of at least four necktie parties from 1851 to 1865. The first victim, William Kendall, swore his innocence, but in those days of swift justice, he was kept hanging.

These trees were used in the old days for hanging people, some guilty, some maybe not.

From the site of hangings we move to the Oregon State Prison, where the old north guard tower was known to be haunted. Guards who were sent to keep watch there always felt that they weren't alone — there was an eerie presence with them in the small room. And no wonder: the tower was built on top of the old prison graveyard (when will they learn?). In 1917 the area was paved over and a recreation yard was installed, and after that the vocational building was put up. Still, the spirits of past inmates roam the area casting a long, dark shadow over a place that knows little joy.

Those still too young for the Big House and just starting a life of crime are sent to Hillcrest, the youth correctional facility. Up on the third floor of the Administration Building is the ghost of an old woman who used to be the housemother in charge of the girls who had been sent there (it was then a girls'

A former housemother still keeps an eye on things at the Hillcrest Youth Correctional Facility. People that have seen her recognize her from old photos.

dormitory). The lady had passed away in the building and now still keeps an eye on things. In an interesting note, old photos of the building and the people who worked there were found, and witnesses to the ghost were able to identify her picture. Even if you don't see her, you'll certainly get a creepy feeling if you're on the third floor — besides which, you'll be in trouble for being in Hillcrest anyway.

The Oregon State Fairgrounds was rumored to be the site of murders and accidental deaths. A local group, Salem Paranormal Investigations, toured the area recently. The location of an accidental hanging was the focus of paranormal activity, and recordings taken there showed signs of electronic voice phenomena, or EVP. Transcripts included a disembodied voice whispering disturbing tidings like "to walk the world is horrible" and "help me, help me up."

Voices from *beyond* have been heard for many years, and attempts to use some sort of technology to capture those sounds have been in use since the turn of the twentieth century at least. In modern terms, EVP is used to describe unexpected voices and sounds that are captured on recording media. What is interesting is that the voices communicate in a language that listeners can understand — their own language. One theory states that the voices need and utilize the vocal chords of the listener (or in fact anyone present in the area), as well as any etheric energy that happens to be present, in order to make communication possible.

A separate place is the Oregon School for the Deaf and it, too, is haunted. A number of years ago in the boy's dorm three of the children went down to the basement, where they were mysteriously killed. Since then a figure in black has been seen a number of times, ghosts have been wandering the boy's and girl's dorms, and there is even talk of a possessed doll. Creepy!

Built by George Guthrie, the Elsinore Theatre was a site of great entertainment. The ghost of Guthrie still looks over the establishment, with a couple of ghostly girls by his side.

The grand Elsinore Theater opened in 1926 and was hailed as "the most beautiful theatre in America" at the time. Created by George B. Guthrie at a cost of $250,000, the building was grand and inspiring by any definition. It seems to be one of the few buildings that have always been used for its original purpose — live entertainment — but that's not all it houses.

The hustle and bustle of performances and rehearsals, the energy, the laughter, the nerves... it has attracted its share of attention from the "other side." There is a certain cold spot on stage, dust comes drifting down from the lighting area even when there is no one there, people can be seen on the scaffolding, and there is always the feeling of someone's eyes on the back of your neck or breathing down your shoulder. A man walks through the seats in the theatre, but above them all is the presence of Guthrie himself, keeping an eye on the stage productions, with a couple of ghostly girls at his side. Far from being the types of spirits who resent intruders, these backstage shades love it when the house is full.

Completely opposite from the wildest place around is the quietest place around, Pioneer Cemetery. Although graveyards have long been held in fear because the silent gray tombstones serve as reminders that death is close by, most psychics agree that the deceased have no reason to haunt the place of their burial. Instead, they prefer to either hang around the location of their death or, much more often, find their energy is drawn to the place they enjoyed most while they were alive. Maybe the

A group of investigators kept hearing sounds coming from inside a crypt at the Pioneer Cemetery.

The Zena Church is very peaceful and has fantastic views across a valley. Still, there are a number of creepy legends about the place.

Salem cemetery is different. A group of paranormal investigators were warned off the site by an angry spirit, and throughout their vigil they heard sounds coming from inside a crypt, footsteps in the night, and a baby crying. They were also able to catch wispy presences on film that weren't visible at the time.

Zena Church and its cemetery outside of Salem are also areas of high supernatural activity. According to local lore, the name "zena" is also the name for a witch. In addition, the church, unlike others, faces away from sunrise. Ghostly spirits wander the church and graveyard at night. Some of the graves are apparently so evil that no grass will grow over them. Other stories tell of a cloaked man who rides back and forth on the church's street, always hiding his face. And, this all adds up to one spooky place.

In this state capitol, even the Governor's Mansion is haunted. The building, called Mahonia Hall, was built in the 1920s by Thomas Lively, who made his millions in the hop business. Although he died at the age of 84, subsequent owners of the

Even the governor isn't immune to ghosts. The mansion is still inhabited by the ghost of the person who built it.

mansion insist he still visits the old place. One person even commented that the black-robed Lively sat on the edge of his bed once or twice a week, looking sad.

Thompson Brewery and Public House has had a number of politicians as regular customers. The building, originally erected as the private home of a Civil War veteran near the turn of the century, has been used for everything from a daycare to a store in its long life. People who work in it now have noticed a resident spirit who shares the home. For instance, one waitress had to brush by a short, gray-haired man in the hallway during a busy night. When she came back, he had vanished, although the room he was in had no exit. He was also seen outside the back of the building where the beer is kept, shyly hiding behind half-open

The Thompson Brewery is a favorite stop for politicians, and was originally built as a house for a Civil War veteran.

The apparition of a small gray haired man has been seen often in this room at the Thompson house.

doors and peeking at workers. In fact, he waves at them to get their attention and then ducks inside the sheds to hide. He was seen through a window once, disappearing in a flash of light.

In a private house that stayed that way is the story of a young man who had the ability to see into the other world. It started with a group of kittens, all of which were black except one white one that soon died. The boy watched his father bury the dead kitten, but a week later he heard it meowing and saw it playing on the stairs. He followed it as it went into the bathroom, but it suddenly disappeared. A number of years later, the boy grew into a young man who began dabbling in the black arts. Once, while in his basement room, he saw an evil entity partially hidden by a door. This was no wispy shadow, but a fully formed menacing person mere feet away from him.

He felt paralyzed as the being stared at him, until he was finally able to move enough to throw a shoe at the door and slam it shut, and then run terrified from the room. On still another occasion, he heard the sound of a woman screaming, and the sounds were coming from within his room. Shortly after this, he started wearing a large crucifix around his neck and the negative energies stopped.

Another malevolent spirit was supposed to haunt Denny's Restaurant. The building has since been torn down. Another ghost, this one of a little girl, is said to haunt the back rooms at the Footlocker store downtown.

Outside of town, on Croisan Creek Road, the specter of a little girl chasing after a ball in the middle of the road can be seen, usually on Friday nights. She is the same one who was killed by a speeding driver taking a corner too sharp. In the Hayesville area a speeding semi will barrel past motorists at night. After it passes, its lights vanish. The same phantom truck also has a habit of blowing its air horn to frighten hitchhikers.

The Mission Mill Museum is not only the site of the 1889 Thomas Kay woolen mill, but also the new home for a number of houses from the pioneer days, including the home of Jason Lee, the founder of Salem. The five-acre complex is also home to a number of ghosts. In the church across the street from the museum, lights have been seen burning brightly at night and a mass was heard being recited, even though the building was empty. There is a bridge near the waterwheel that drives the mill. On it a woman can be seen running from her husband who had murdered her on the very spot many years ago. In the mill itself, an angry presence can be felt next to the turbine. No wonder, since one worker lost his life maintaining the engine while it was running. It's not all pain

The ghosts of an accident victim, a murder victim, and a happy worker have all been seen at the Mission Mill.

and anguish at the mill, though. If you keep an eye open you may see an old groundskeeper named Wayne who still likes to putter around the place, keeping his hand in, although he's been dead quite a while.

Sherwood

This small town has an interesting white corner house, complete with white picket fence. This is the house where a midwife used to ply her trade. Now, many locals have seen a little girl in a white dress walk into the house and disappear. On the same block is a storeowner whose aunt could not only see ghosts, but also knew exactly when any relative, near or far, was dying. She would be washing dishes and then suddenly say "aunt so-and-so has just passed away. The family needs me." Then she would pack up and leave.

Many locals have seen a little girl in a white dress walk into this house and simply disappear.

Siletz

The town of Siletz in Lincoln County is named after the local Native Americans, the Siletz Indians. One of their members haunts this area, and he's known as Whistleman. He was a little, old non-descript Indian with baggy pants. People would see him walking along the road as they drove past, and yet, four miles or so down the road they would see him again, walking in the same direction! He was known and feared by the local natives as Owlman, a shaman of great power who could turn himself into an owl at the drop of a hat. They would leave offerings of fish out for him, because nobody wanted to hear his owl hoot — that meant death was not far behind. Some say he would shamble along in the center of town, muttering "Whistleman's gonna get ya!"

There is a bridge on a certain section of road near this town. On dark, wet nights, when the wind is howling, a Klamath Indian lady can be seen on it. According to legend, she either jumped off the bridge with her child, or was pushed off by her enraged husband. In any event, if you stop and pick her up, she'll sit quietly in the back of the car and eventually disappear altogether. However, those who callously pass her by will surely crash.

One couple had camped at Moonshine Park in Siletz. Their site was on a clifftop overlooking the clear flowing Siletz River. In the evening, they were startled by the sound of branches snapping, but thought nothing of it and soon decided to turn in for the night. The husband walked to the park's bathrooms, but when he returned to the campsite he noticed his wife peering at the river with a flashlight, saying, "What is that?" Soon they both witnessed a strange being in the water, human shaped, except in place of hands it had claws with three fingers on each claw. It also had large eyes that covered nearly half its head, which was bullet shaped. The entire body was covered in brown hair. However, the most disconcerting thing was the casual, completely unafraid way it looked up at the pair as it slowly floated in the water. The pair watching it felt exactly the opposite and spent a terrified night in the truck instead of their tent.

Springfield

For being one of the larger towns, Springfield appears to have relatively few ghosts, but the ones that are there are interesting.

At the corner of Daisy Street and South 49th Street near the railroad tracks you can call up a ghost if you follow the correct procedure. Five people are needed to sit in the shape of a pentagram, which is best performed between 11 p.m. and 1 a.m. Then, while recording the event on a tape machine, ask if there is anyone there, and to give you a sign. Suddenly a man will appear with a flashlight and will say something along the order of "I can see you, and I just wanted to let you know that I'm here," and then will vanish. So that's a fun family project.

During the 1960s a family that moved into a rental house found an old trunk in the attic, which they moved from its location and excitedly opened but found empty. Later in the evening they heard the sounds of footsteps in the attic, and when they investigated found that the lid of the trunk that they had closed was now open. Each night the sound of footsteps would return, and the lid of the trunk would either be opened or closed, whatever was opposite to the way they had left it. Sometimes the sounds were so loud they had to turn on music to drown it out. They finally decided (why did it take them so long?) to move the trunk back to its original location, and then the noises stopped.

At another rented house, a young family (father, mother, and son) moved in...only to find that the son refused to go upstairs because of the specter of a man he had seen in the bathroom. Other paranormal events included books going missing. In one instance, the pair had been searching for a particular book on their bookshelf. They would go over each title together, slowly, back and forth, even saying the names of the titles out loud, only to turn up empty-handed. And then suddenly the book would be found, in plain sight, right on the end of the shelf. Their smoke alarms would go off, but made the beeping sounds very slowly. Even though the neighborhood they lived in was a nice one, violence was occurring with more frequency, leaving them to wonder if there was a vestige of negative psychic energy still floating in the area.

In between the towns of Eugene and Springfield is an area known as Marcola. At the end of a fairly spooky road is a small cemetery that has a reputation for being very haunted. Supposedly it was built on Native American burial or hunting grounds—and we all know what happens after that! There is an imposing house sitting near the cemetery that features a pair of stone lions at the front gate. When investigators were standing at the gate, they felt very uncomfortable, maybe because the home was rumored to harbor a monstrous ghostly entity and a large black dog with glowing red eyes. However, as hair-raising as those sounds are, it's the very intense, heavy negative feeling that saturates the area that frightens most people away, as if something very old and sinister still lurks in the shadows of the tombstones.

In the cemetery itself an old man can be seen walking along, but then suddenly vanishes. The snarling of the black dog can be heard, as well as the squeaking of a rocking chair.

The local newspaper, *The Springfield News*, was itself the home to a ghost. Here is an account of one eyewitness:

I was working in the Composing Department of the *Springfield News* one day (this was about 2002), when I saw someone out of the corner of my eye waiting to talk to me. It looked like a woman with shoulder-length wavy blonde hair. When I looked up to talk to her, there was no one there. I looked down again at my worktable and there she was again. Looked up...no one there. It happened once more. I thought it was kind of odd, but dismissed it, being busy with my work.

A few days later, we were having an employee meeting in the adjoining room. There was a big poster on one table that featured a compilation of former employees. One of the photos caught my eye. It looked just like the person who had been trying to get my attention a few days earlier. I pointed to the picture of the person (who was actually a man with shoulder-length wavy blonde hair in the style of the early 1970s) and asked Mark, a pressman who had been working there for over thirty years, who the person was. He said, "That's our resident ghost." I must have shown surprise on my face because he asked me if I had seen him. I said I thought that I had, and told him about the incident a few days earlier. He didn't seem surprised and told me that the man, Steve, was a pressman who had worked there back in the '70s. He said Steve was a fun guy, but was a bit wild; a partier who liked to play practical jokes. Mark said one night Steve left work on his motorcycle and was killed in an accident on the freeway when he was hit by a semi-truck.

This incident got a lot of us talking about ghosts at the *Springfield News*. The editor at the time, Anne Seales, said she had heard footsteps many times when she was the only one working late. She seemed to think another former employee, Brad, was responsible for the footsteps and also for ceiling tiles being pulled down on other occasions. She told us that Brad had worked there about the same time as Steve and they partied together. Brad had gone through a recovery program from drug addiction and was getting himself together when one night he didn't show up to work. His co-workers were worried about him because they couldn't reach him by phone, so someone went to his house only to find out that Brad had died the night before from an accidental drug overdose.

Several times when my supervisor Kathryn and myself were working there late we would hear sounds of someone walking around upstairs. We would leave the building and call the police, thinking someone might have gotten inside. They would search the entire building, but never found anyone. Kathryn also said that she had seen a man dressed in very old-style clothing with tall hat walking down the "haunted hallway," the hallway that led to the women's bathroom that gave just about everyone there the creeps. Kathryn said he would go to the end of the hallway and turn the corner, disappearing at that point. *The Springfield News* had been a newspaper in that building way back to before 1900, so there would have been people dressed that way working there.

One time a co-worker, Michelle, came running out of the darkroom. She looked very frightened and wouldn't go back in there alone. She said it felt like someone was watching her there. I went in with her while we processed the film, and it was indeed a very creepy atmosphere in there. Another time Michelle came back from the women's bathroom with something in her hand. She dropped it on the table in front of me. It was an old nametag with "Steve" stamped on it. There were no employees at the time we were there named Steve. Maybe this was one of his practical jokes?

The publisher at the time, Doris Towery, called a Shaman and had him come in to do a ceremony. She asked Kathryn, Michelle, and myself to be present. She didn't want us to talk about it to co-workers as she said many of them were very religious and wouldn't approve of the ceremony. The shaman came into the newspaper one day and performed a cleansing ceremony. He asked me to drum for the ceremony and he went into a semi-trance and contacted Brad and Steve. He told them they were deceased and they needed to leave the earthly plane. He then proceeded to show Brad and Steve how to go towards the light. The spirit known as Steve even asked if he could ride his motorcycle. During the ceremony, most of us heard crackling noises like a fire makes.

🍁 🍁 🍁 🍁 🍁

Another reminiscence from the psychic Heather comes from the Thurston area of Springfield:

It was in a two-bedroom pink house with a large yard. I don't remember too much about it, but the voices I will never forget. I was always hearing voices there, someone calling the name Tina. I didn't know a Tina, and neither did my family. I would hear what seemed like conversations that were garbled. I told my parents about them, but they dismissed them as an overactive imagination.

Not too long after that I met a friend. Her name was Tiffany and I would sit and play with my LiteBrite toy with her for hours. The only problem was that my parents couldn't see her. I remember her perfectly: pigtails, sweet smile, and a sundress. My parents said she was my imaginary friend, and that she wasn't real, but I remember her being very real. Now I realize that she was a ghost. I'm not sure if she died there, or what, but her dress seemed outdated.

Sunriver Hotel

This hotel is situated on the site of the former Army camp, Camp Adair. One of the soldiers who had been training there for World War II was accidentally killed, and now he stays at the hotel, where he can be seen in his long military coat pacing the upper balcony, sometimes tossing objects and playing other pranks if the mood suits him.

Tillamook

This town is famous in Oregon for its great cheese. It also has a couple of other items it's known for, as we shall see.

During certain stormy nights, waves crash hard against the jagged rocks that surround the Tilamook Lighthouse. Any ship caught in this storm will be in great peril. Sure enough, the keepers in the lighthouse watch helplessly as a decrepit old ship is seen, pulled closer and closer into the rocks. They can see the crew fight desperately to steer the ship away, but to no avail, and soon it's beaten to a pulp against the cliff. When the storm finally dies down, the keepers are sent to look for the wreckage and dead crew. Nothing is found. In fact, nothing is ever found as this scenario is played out again and again by the same phantom ship.

One of the roads leading into the lush Tillamook valley is Agaard Road. If you travel this highway in the small hours of the morning, you can find a man named Lazlo in his flannel shirt smoking a pipe, contentedly fishing the creek that runs under the road. His wife can be seen across the

A horrible shipwreck with great loss of life has occurred over and over again near Tillamook Lighthouse.

street, waiting impatiently with an annoyed expression on her face. The lights are on in their house, with a wispy trail of smoke rising from the chimney, even though it hasn't been lived in for over ten years.

On the same stretch of road, a young boy in blue shorts can be found near an old swimming hole in the creek. Joey, as the locals call him, is usually seen in the summer. He appears blue in the face with water dripping from him. His pathetic calls for his "mommy and daddy" have made people follow him, but he always disappears before he gets to the highway.

Chapter Eleven

Wandering Souls

Welches

This little town had nothing to do with grape juice, but everything to do with ghosts.

In the town there was a small wicker casket on display. These were made in the old days as temporary caskets for viewing the body before interment. This one was for a child, and ever since it was put on display, the ghost of a little girl could be seen wandering around the area.

Another case in town is that of a former innkeeper, a woman who became the lover of an escaped convict. She kept him hidden in one of the rooms, but as is often the case, one day he left and never came back. Distraught, she jumped out of the second-story window to her death, and now lingers on. There are other spirits in the area of the hotel, too, and no wonder, since it was built on an Indian burial ground.

West Linn

The paper mill in this town was once a flourmill. Apparently catacombs had been excavated beneath the mill, and many people had been injured over the years. The rooms have since been abandoned. It sounds like the workers are still working even when they're dead, because a janitor once heard disembodied voices asking, "What time is it? Let's go home." The clock on the wall is stuck at the 5 p.m. position. In the afterlife, is it always near quitting time?

Wheeler

This quaint former fishing village is the site of the Old Wheeler Hotel with its lovely views over Nehalem Bay. According to the owner and others, the place is haunted. Sometimes you can see a presence just out of the corner of your eye, but when you look, the form is gone. Once, the owner was looking in a mirror and saw the reflection of someone sitting in a chair. He turned to look at the unknown man, but the chair was empty. Sort of a reverse-vampire situation. Ghost hunters have also visited the hotel, taking photos of orbs outside the basement.

As many people know, the surest way to stir up supernatural activity is to make renovations to old buildings. Former inhabitants now in spirit are like the dust on a windowsill, and remain there quiet and contented throughout the long years. When change is afoot, these energies become disturbed and agitated, awakening from their slumber in a foul mood. This happened to the owners as they spent large amounts of time and money trying to bring the old hotel back to its former glory. When they started on the project, it seemed as though some force was trying to block their progress, with disaster after disaster occurring. Finally, the building — or the entities in it — decided to accept the changes and things were fine from then on.

Another home beset by bad spirits was actually burned down by its owner, a woman descended from a local Indian tribe. According to legend, a native child had died in a fire in that very spot many years in the past. The woman had no intention of ever rebuilding the home. With all this psychic energy whirling around, it's lucky that some of it has spilled over in positive ways. Many in the town feel that there is good energy, especially the type that results in lucky coincidences that wind up helping others in some way.

Yaquina Head Lighthouse

This is the tallest lighthouse in Oregon, and something spooky inhabits the tall circular stairway leading up to the lantern. According to some accounts, a keeper named Higgins either got drunk, fell, and broke his neck on the stairs or was forced to work on the lamp in nasty conditions when he was very ill. In any case, he died as the result, and his co-worker refused to go on the staircase at night because of his presence.

Another death near the lighthouse resulted in more hauntings. In this scenario, a lighthouse keeper was drowned as he tried to cross a creek near the building, and his daughter was so upset she shot herself. It's her ghost that can be seen wandering the beaches nearby.

Yoncalla

At the very end of Applegate Road, lying at the bottom of a hill, sits the Applegate house, so haunted it's a wonder there is any room for the living inside its walls. Anyone staying there has heard the usual thumps, bumps, and footsteps common among older haunted homes. People have also heard the swish of skirts, babies crying, and people arguing. They've even heard banjos and fiddles playing. Others have seen a woman wearing a white dress, another woman and a man in baggy pants. A chair can be seen rocking by itself. If you're looking for a good night's sleep, this probably isn't the place.

Another home, this one an old farmhouse, features a baby's cradle that has been passed down from generation to generation. The cradle is so used to rocking that it does it all by itself now, or is it the ghost of the young girl rocking her baby brother?

Chapter Twelve

The Serpent, Sasquatch, & Other Creatures

The greater Willamette Valley area is situated perfectly between the ocean on the west and the mountains on the east. Both of these areas offer abundant natural resources and great beauty. They also harbor strange creatures that are rarely seen, but have made the area home longer than any man. The rocky Oregon coast has been the location for sightings of sea monsters for many years. These sightings of creatures resembling giant eels, enormous squid, and Loch Ness Monster type animals occur along the entire wild coast. Area natives have known about these monsters for hundreds of years, but the first ones to be mentioned in print have only been in the past hundred years or so.

One of the first sightings recorded concerned a creature that was nicknamed Claude, which was first seen in 1934 near the mouth of the Columbia River. Described as having a large round body, long neck, coarse gray fur, an evil, snake-like (or sometimes horse-like) head and being about forty feet in length, it was spotted off and on for the next twenty years. Besides Claude, another serpent named Marvin the Monster

A sea serpent named Claude used to be seen at the mouth of the Columbia River. According to eyewitness reports at the time, it bore a remarkable resemblance to the Loch Ness Monster.

has been observed since the 1960s. The creature was even recorded on video, swimming with a corkscrew motion in 180 feet of water, with the footage studied by marine biologists. Like many water monsters, the ones seen off the coast and in lakes are usually dark green to brown in color, often shiny, but sometimes exhibiting scales and even fur. Most have been described as having a head like a horse.

Other strange sea creatures include a twelve-foot cow-like animal that was covered in hair; a thirty-foot long sea serpent with the usual snake-like head and a fan-shaped tail that was seen frolicking in the water close to a number of reliable witnesses; and Old Hairy, a hairy monster about twenty-two feet long that washed ashore, again with a cow-like body, but also sporting nine tails. The beast weighed over 1,000 pounds. Expert opinions varied from its being a whale shark to elasmobranch to something prehistoric.

A number of lakes have long been known to harbor monsters by the native peoples. In at least two lakes, Crater and Crescent, non-natives have also seen the huge dark shapes of something in the deep, as panicking fish roiled the water around them.

Sasquatch

Western Oregon is home to hundreds of thousands of acres of deep, green montane forests, often shrouded in a cloak of fog—and most of it rarely seen by humans. This is the domain of the North American Sasquatch, or Bigfoot, as it is commonly known. According to many experts, the Sasquatch is a throwback to ancient times, not unlike other supposedly extinct animals that have since been discovered. It may even be a form of early humans known as Gigantapithecus, which might have followed the migration patterns of large prey animals across the land bridge that once connected Russia to Alaska, and from there southwards to the Northwest (and eventually most other states).

This large, hairy man-like creature has lived in the remote woods since then, staying well away from man whenever possible. Sasquatches are known for their smell — awful; like a wet dog and garbage rolled into one, enormous height of six to ten feet, huge barrel chest, extra long arms that reach below the knee, and, obviously, large feet. The hair that covers almost all of their bodies is described as dark brown to black to reddish in color (and sometimes even white). It is much shorter to non-existent on the face, palms of the hands, and soles of the feet. The facial area features a large jaw, pronounced

Between six and ten feet tall, weighing hundreds of pounds, and covered in thick hair, Bigfoot or sasquatches, have been *seen*, *heard*, and *smelled* ever since white settlers came to Oregon, and by the Natives before that.

canines, protruding brow with dark eyes ending in a conical ridge at the peak. Although they exhibit characteristics of both humans and apes, they are more closely related to humans, a fact that wasn't lost on a few people that have had them in their gun sight and were unable to pull the trigger, feeling that they would be committing murder.

They communicate through grunts, howls, whistles, and a peculiar jabbering talk that the natives of long ago could apparently understand. Sasquatch will also pound sticks against trees to communicate over long distances, and mark their territory by breaking the tops off of trees and erecting piles of stones. Their diet is close to that of the bear that shares its habitat and resources. They eat a variety of plant matter, seeds and berries, lichen, insects, and grubs, as well as small animals. They have also been observed hunting large game animals by simply chasing them down and breaking the necks of their prey.

Sasquatch nests of flattened branches and ferns have been found, but most inhabit hidden caves, a few of which have been found and investigated. One cave in particular was strewn with animal bones and in a corner was a pile of animal skins made into a rudimentary bed. Although they have been seen to use basic clubs, they have no knowledge of fire.

Because of their size, skeptics wonder why no skeleton has ever been found. For one thing, these creatures might have burial rites much as early man did, and possibly hide the bodies deep in caves or in the bottom of ponds and lakes. Furthermore, hardly any skeletons of animals are ever found in the deep forest, because many other animals such as porcupines and raccoons have a craving for the calcium in the bones and so they are disposed of rather quickly. For instance, there are millions of squirrels hopping around in the trees, but how often have you seen a squirrel skeleton?

If anyone wants to think that the giant hairy man of the Northwest woods is a recent invention, they should listen to what the Native Americans of the area have to say about the creature. They feel he is more man than animal; in fact, they call him an Indian. Known variously as yayaya-ash (frightener) or ste-yeh-hah' mah (spirit hiding under cover of the woods), the most common name is Stick Indian, for its habit of throwing sticks or poking them into dwellings.

According to tales from the elders, they are like big, hairy Indians who live in the remote high altitudes of the Cascades, where they sleep during the day in camouflaged caves or deep within the forest undergrowth. If an Indian lagged too far behind in a hunting party, he might hear a strange bird whistle off to one side. Soon, the whistle would sound from another side, then far ahead, and then behind—until the traveler was thoroughly confused and dropped unconscious from exhaustion and stress. Upon awakening, he could consider himself lucky that only his clothes and hunting supplies have been stolen. In fact, just being in their vicinity often causes people to become dizzy, light-headed, and faint. The Stick Indians are known for their lightning speed and great endurance (like Sasquatch), and annoying habit of kidnapping young children and women. In other words, they're definitely to be avoided because of their nasty nature, although one native told how just as he was going to sleep under a blanket in the woods, two Stick Indians walked up and without a word, settled in to sleep on either side of him!

Tales of Sasquatch by Native Americans go back at least three hundred years, with the hairy man of the woods being thought of as no less living than a bear or deer, although sightings of them were thought to be great omens. The natives have a live and let live attitude toward Bigfoot. A number of years ago, my girlfriend and I were staying with friends in northwest Washington State many years ago. At night, we could hear a strange, plaintive howling that started low and ended in a high, lonesome note. I've heard plenty of coyotes, wolves, and mountain lions before in Montana, and wondered what kind of animal could make that sound. Our Native host told us that it was Sasquatch, who often called at night. They even pointed out the remote canyon they lived in, and warned us not to camp there, because the Sasquatch didn't like it. Being young and foolish, that's exactly what we did.

As we hiked in about two miles, a busy creek was flashing along one side, and tall hills covered in an impenetrable thicket of trees hemmed us in on either side. We felt nothing out of the ordinary and soon found an ideal spot to camp at, in a small meadow. We fished for our dinner, pitched our tent, and went to sleep when the sun went down. I can't be sure how long we slept, but in the middle of the night we were woken by the sounds of grunts, short hoots, and a scary vocalization that sounded like very fast mumbling outside the tent. At first they came from the direction of the nearby hills, but then suddenly the sounds surrounded us. I unzipped the tent and looked out cautiously with a flashlight, but couldn't see anything. I quickly dove back in the tent while we talked about what to do. Then short sticks and rocks were being thrown and bouncing off the tent fabric. The grunts and hoots grew louder and more menacing. Finally, we realized that we could smell a terrible odor like wet garbage and there could be no pretending that we had incurred the wrath of the local sasquatches. We put our boots on and after psyching each other up, dove out of the tent and ran in the total darkness the entire two miles back to the country road where we left our car. We got in, locked the doors and only returned to the campground reluctantly the next day to retrieve our gear.

We didn't find any footprints, but we did see sticks and rocks in a ring around the tent. Some people have suggested that our Indian friends were playing a trick on us. But we know what we saw, heard, and most importantly, smelled. Once you've come into contact with *The Other*, whether it's a ghost, UFO, or even Sasquatch, nothing can shake your faith.

In the southern part of Oregon, by Grant's Pass, a trucker was traveling on an almost deserted road when he saw something dark and hairy lying in the road. He felt sure he was going to run over it, but when he was almost on the point of impact, a large, very heavy and hairy thing ran in front of the truck, grabbed the sleeping being on the road, and took off into the night. On another occasion, a man and his wife were driving up a logging road in the backcountry. When they reached a certain spot, they stopped the truck and rolled down the windows to look at the scenery. Suddenly something was throwing rocks at them, followed by a blood curdling scream and the sounds of trees being snapped. Another unhappy Sasquatch.

Many sightings happen along lonely roadways, since that's about the only place that a person and a sasquatch would be likely to meet. For instance, in the coastal area of Coos County two people were driving a Jeep out of a forest. The vehicle had powerful lights, and they suddenly shone on a large hairy man, with long black and smoky colored hair and blue eyes. Although the creature was standing in a three-foot ditch, it still came to eye level with the riders in the Jeep. Unusually, the witnesses didn't feel frightened.

At a campground near the town of Glide, a Sasquatch was seen by over a dozen campers as the nine-foot creature calmly walked across a clearing, swinging its arms as it went. Half the campers left the area that night. People aren't the only things to be scared by it. In another wilderness area close by, a couple was walking with their German Shepherds when they saw a very large brown creature walking through the thick undergrowth. The dogs chased the creature until they were out of sight, but soon came running back, terrified. There was a strong musky odor in the air. On a logging road near the town of Yoncalla, two elk hunters saw a large, very dark brown creature walking on two legs. It started at them for a while, and when it turned to leave they noticed a smaller creature, about five feet tall and lighter in color, walking beside it.

One family has had many encounters with sasquatches while spending time in a remote campground near Roseburg. They have seen as many as nine in a group and watched them walk down a road in a line, tallest to smallest. They even left a candy bar for one who ate it, wrapper and all. They claim the Sasquatch adult to be about eight feet tall, very muscular, with short black hair covering the entire body except the face, hands, and feet, which resemble leather. The family claims the sasquatches were just as curious of them as they were of the creatures, and even called for legislation banning the killing of a Bigfoot.

Another great encounter with a Sasquatch also comes from the Roseburg area. Two people who were exploring for Indian artifacts came upon a cave in the woods. There was soft pumice at the mouth of the cave and a large number of giant tracks could be seen. Entering the cave with flashlights they found a number of animal skins with the hair on lying in piles, presumably for bedding. There were many animal bones scattered around the freshly killed carcass of a deer. Whatever had killed the deer had rolled the hide back off the body of the animal and cut (or chewed) it off. There was an overpowering awful odor in the cave, and no sign of fire or tools. Upon returning to the cave another day, they happened upon the Sasquatch itself, which came within three feet of the pair. They described it as being over seven feet tall, covered with short shaggy hair, but having a smooth face. The cave has since been covered by a rockslide.

In Lane County, two hunters stumbled upon a Sasquatch that was bent over a deer carcass. It stood up and stared at them for a long while, until one of the hunters started to aim a .22 at the creature. The other hunter wouldn't let him shoot, and with that the Sasquatch slung the deer over its shoulder and walked off. In fact, Sasquatch sightings have occurred in almost every county in western Oregon. It dislikes having humans in its presence and can easily make anyone feel unwelcome. Finally, it can really leave an odor when it wants to, although this isn't always the case, and so it seems likely that the overpowering wet dog/garbage smell is used as a warning. Contrary to popular belief, there is plenty of evidence of Sasquatch, including footprints, handprints, hair samples, nesting sites, and recorded sounds. However, these samples can only be measured against other known samples. For instance a hair sample can be proven that it's not human and not simian since there are plenty of known specimens of them to measure against, but cannot be proven to be of a Sasquatch because there are no certain examples of that type of hair.

In the spring of 2002, three friends were driving on an old road near the highest mountain in the Oregon Coast range when their way was stopped by downed trees lying across the road. Since they were in no hurry, they got out and walked around and soon came upon a track that featured five toes about fifteen inches in length. Excited, they followed the tracks as they went uphill. One of the group went back to the truck to retrieve a camera as the others kept scouting, soon finding a second set of tracks, smaller than the first but running parallel to it. The group never saw what made the tracks, but did hear some very unusual calls in the deeply wooded areas near the road.

The Applegate Bigfoot Trap

Located near Applegate Lake, which is about a half-hour from Medford, is possibly the only Bigfoot trap in the country. The trap, created by Ron Olson and his father in 1974, was built to hopefully capture one of the elusive creatures alive. According to Olson, the trap was only meant to contain the Sasquatch long enough to be scientifically observed. The pair had a tranquilizer gun, manacles and a large sled just for that purpose.

The huge trap is basically a 10' x 10' box made of sturdy planks which are bound together with steel bands and anchored to the spot with telephone poles sunk into the ground. A heavy metal grate served as the trap door. However, since curious hikers frequently visit the site, the Forest Service bolted the door open in 1980 to prevent any accidental incarcerations. The structure had been badly damaged over the years but was recently restored by volunteers in the Forest Service's Passport in Time program.

Olson, who was a wildlife film distributor in the Sixties got his first taste of Bigfoot when he met and worked with Roger Patterson, undoubtedly the most well-known of all Sasquatch hunters (he was the person who filmed the famous "Bigfoot walking along a creek bed" footage). The pair wanted to make a documentary about the hominid, and in the course of research for the film Olson investigated nearly three hundred sightings, some misidentifications, some hoaxes, some real.

One story in particular concerned a miner named Perry who had found very large human-like tracks in his garden. Although Perry died before Olson had a chance to interview him, stories about the miner still circulated. He told how the Bigfoot would come into the area in the fall. He could look across a canyon and watch them.

To date, the trap has managed to catch two bears.

Chapter Thirteen

UFOs

Oregon has seen its share of strange objects in the sky ever since Kenneth Arnold's famous sighting in nearby Washington State of what was later termed "flying saucers" over Mt. Rainier in 1947. Close to a thousand other sightings have been reported since then, and most likely there are many more that have gone unreported. In fact, stories of flying saucers, and especially of the bright, silvery kind, started in Washington and Oregon and spread to all the other states. The greater Willamette Valley has been the focus for some very interesting activity over the years.

One of the most recent concerns what at first appeared to be a falling star near a place called Rice Hill, south of Eugene. However, the object traced a "J" pattern in the sky, which meteors have never been known to do. In another case, two witnesses near the town of Lebanon saw a silver disc appear through low clouds. It then vanished into the air. In Eugene itself, two more witnesses watched for fifteen minutes as two bright objects moved through the sky, before flashing brightly and blinking out. It was during the early evening and still quite light outside.

A large, triangular-shaped UFO was seen by several witnesses hovering close to the highway near Fern Ridge Reservoir.

One of the most terrifying UFO events occurred on the road between Eugene and Veneta, close to an area well known for mysterious phenomena — Fern Ridge Lake. It began as a blinking red light that would hover over the lake, dip down, and hover again. As the witnesses drove further, they noticed that cars had pulled off the road on both sides to stare at the object. By now it was much closer, hovering about thirty feet in the air, so it was easy to get a detailed description of the craft. It was large, triangular, and black, with three shiny metal discs that spun rapidly on each corner. Inside the discs were very bright lights. A dome was situated in the center (on the bottom). The tall grass under the object was waving wildly from the force of the UFO, which was strangely silent.

During the 1970s, an equally strange encounter took place near Coos Bay. In this case a man was driving with his wife and child from Oregon to California. He had to take a detour on a hillside because of a landslide and noticed three lights in formation that appeared below him. He pulled over and got out of the car to have a better look at the lights, when he suddenly walked right into the side of the craft. It was surfaced with some sort of material that soaked in light, and the craft was the same general shape as a submarine, but with a slightly darker color underneath, where it was flatter. Using a flashlight, the man found that the material had a sparkly appearance when viewed close up. He then saw that the lights were in fact domes or portals made of a crystal-like material, probably eight feet across and twelve feet high. He finally noticed with a shock that the bottom of the craft was at his shoulder level, with nothing holding it up! It didn't make any noise, didn't hum or vibrate, but was rigid in its position off the ground. After viewing it for another few minutes, the man heard a scurrying sound in the nearby bushes, finally panicked, and ran back to his car.

In 1959 a UFO was spotted at Redmond Airport. A number of witnesses saw it, including some using binoculars. A white object was seen falling and then hovering two hundred feet to the ground. The object then began to grow larger and brighter, enough to illuminate the trees in the area. Finally, it changed hue to a dull red and moved off. The UFO was detected on radar and jets were scrambled to intercept. As the jets approached, the object emitted streams of yellow and orange lights from beneath and rose into the clouds. It was later reported again about twenty-five miles away.

In 2007, a couple towing a trailer filmed a UFO for several minutes while driving near Medford. It was of the classic silver-metallic disc shape, and was easily distinguished from an aircraft because the couple had also recorded one on the same tape.

One woman was leaving the Salem area with her young son in the car. As they drove, she heard a low humming or throbbing kind of sound. Looking out the car window, she was astonished to see a bright group of flashing white lights that formed a triangle. Her son saw the craft, as did a couple walking along the street. It was flying, or hovering, very low in the sky and moving at a slow speed. At her first opportunity, she called her husband, who had also gone outside to find the source of the mysterious sound. When she got home, all three stood outside and watched the lights travel off into the distance.

A couple was in their bedroom in the morning when they saw a brightly colored, orange oval shaped object whiz past their window. As they looked at each other, the object zoomed past the window again, retracing its steps.

One female office worker went outside her workplace on a rainy day and was surprised to see a vertical column of glowing spheres, with each individual sphere bobbing and weaving up and down inside the column. She persuaded a couple of coworkers to investigate the strange formation, but for some reason, they didn't register the slightest interest!

At the height of the UFO craze — in 1947 — Oregon residents had many encounters. In Astoria, located at the mouth of the Columbia River and the Pacific Ocean, a housewife phoned to report a bright flying disc flying over the military base of Fort Stevens. In the 1940s people weren't quite as enlightened as we are now, and the authorities demanded to hear from a man instead. Soon enough, the woman found a welder who had also seen the craft. He stated that he watched the flying saucer through his welding goggles because the light was so intense.

Sightings of very thin, white flying objects, traveling very fast at an altitude of 10,000 feet above the Portland area was reported not only by many people on the ground, but by the crew of a United Airlines plane flying at the same height. Between two to twenty of the larger UFOs were observed for about ten minutes. The first people to spot the craft were the police, with a number of patrol cars calling in sightings. The Harbor Patrol also spotted a number of the discs that were bobbing erratically and moving at an incredible rate.

Shades of Close Encounters! A woman and her husband were driving along the outskirts of Roseburg in the early 1970s when suddenly a blinding white light engulfed the car. The next thing she knew, they were five miles down the road, driving like crazy, and scared to death as the UFO continued to follow them until they got to the house they were staying in and ran inside. The missing time between their first encounter and entering the house has never been accounted for.

A sighting from the air was made by a woman passenger on a plane flying from Las Vegas to Portland. As they neared Mount Hood, cruising at an altitude of about 30,000 feet on a crystal clear day, she looked out her window to see three circular white discs flying in close formation below them, at around 10,000 feet. They were moving very fast but were much too small to be jets. Amazingly, as a frequent flyer, she had seen a single white flying disc in the same general vicinity a few years in the past.

Another pretty close encounter occurred in Salem as a couple was driving home from a shopping trip in town.

Something unusual must have made the husband look out into the cloudless, starry night. It turned out to be a light hovering above the road, something that could have been a helicopter, except that it made no sound. His wife was staring at it as well, and after a few moments they decided to drive home. However, as they neared the parking lot of their apartment complex, they were frightened to see the craft hovering about fifty feet off the ground, directly in front of them — it had tailed them home! At this distance, it was easy to tell that the craft was a gray triangular shaped affair, thirty feet wide, with lights running around the edge. It was able to hover motionless, with only the slightest humming sound. The couple ran inside the comparative safety of their home and watched as the craft slowly floated away.

Arguably the most famous UFO event after the Kenneth Arnold sightings was the sighting, and resulting photos, taken by a Mrs. Trent at her farm in McMinnville during the month of May in 950. In fact, the photos are still hotly debated today. As the story goes, Mrs. Trent was outside feeding her rabbits when she noticed a disc-shaped UFO approaching from the northeast. She called her husband Paul to see the craft and he then ran inside to retrieve his camera. Back outside, he took one shot, then wound the film, and fired off another a few minutes later. He didn't even bother to get the film developed until he had used up the rest of the roll.

The local bank displayed the two UFO photos, which in turn attracted the attention of a local newspaper reporter, who filed a story on the encounter. That story was picked up by the nationals, and it was featured in the June issue of *Life* magazine in 1950. The photos were examined and found to be authentic.

Epilogue

We have seen over the course of this book a large number of hauntings. Some are by spirits seen, some unseen but felt. Some are very frightening, while others have been comforting to witnesses. Many visitations have happened in private homes or buildings and because of that, I have had to keep their locations general in nature. However, there are still quite a few that are happily open to the public and can be visited by those with a curious nature. The Willamette Valley, with its seemingly spook-tastic combination of fog, mists, water and wild areas, doesn't have more or less hauntings than other places. Any place where people make their homes will eventually wind up having some of the inhabitants linger on after death, but of course, this area of the country has only been populated by non-natives since around the middle of the 1800s, so maybe it needs time to build up a big backlog of the deceased to really make its mark on the world.

Ghost hunting in general is at an all time high, with new paranormal investigation groups forming every day. Many shows on television and radio are concerned with ferreting out spirits, and there are thousands of websites devoted to the topic. Modern technology has made much of it possible from a technological standpoint, and there is a growing public demand for more information. We can feel that we're hanging on the cusp of something very big, as the violent regimes of old slowly fade (kicking and screaming) and a new sensibility comes into being, a sense of being one people, world citizens. Outmoded ways of thinking, like scientific empiricism, are cast off as the scientists themselves discover that on a nano-level, everyone, and everything, is interconnected (surprising, just as native peoples have been telling us for ages). Archaeological studies have shown that everyone on Earth is descended genetically from one female, an actual Eve.

We have discovered so much, and yet there are still unexplained shadows that flit across our rooms, mysterious shapes that loom up from the deep; strange beings walk the remote forests and otherworldly visitors silently patrol the night skies. May there always be something... unexplained.

Glossary

Air Probe Thermometer

A thermometer with an external probe that is capable of taking instant measurements of the air temperature.

Anomalous field

A field that cannot be explained or ruled out by various possibilities; which can be a representation of spirit or paranormal energy present.

Apparition

A transparent form of a human or animal; a spirit.

Artificial field

A field that is caused by electrical outlets, appliances, etc.

Aural Enhancer

A listening device that enhances or amplifies audio signals. i.e., Orbitor Bionic Ear.

Automatic writing

The act of a spirit guiding a human agent in writing a message that is brought through by the spirit.

Base readings

These are the readings taken at the start of an investigation and are used as a means of comparing other readings taken later during the course of the investigation.

Demonic Haunting
A haunting that is caused by an inhuman or subhuman energy or spirit.

Dowsing Rods
A pair of L-shaped rods or a single Y-shaped rod, used to detect the presence of what the person using them is trying to find.

Electro-static generator
A device that electrically charges the air; it's often used in paranormal investigations/research as a means to contribute to the materialization of paranormal or spiritual energy.

ELF/EMF
Extremely Low Frequency / Electro Magnetic Field

ELF Meter/EMF Meter
A device that measures electric and magnetic fields.

EVP
Electronic Voice Phenomena.

False positive
Something that is being interpreted as paranormal within a picture or video and is, in fact, a natural occurrence or defect of the equipment used.

Gamera
A 35mm film camera connected with a motion detector that is housed in a weatherproof container and takes a picture when movement is detected. Made by Silver Creek Industries.

Geiger Counter
A device that measures gamma and x-ray radiation.

Infra Red
An invisible band of radiation at the lower end of the visible light spectrum. With wavelengths from 750 nm to 1 mm, infrared starts at the end of the microwave spectrum and ends at the beginning of visible light. Infrared transmission typically requires an unobstructed line of sight between transmitter and receiver. Widely used in most audio and video remote controls, infrared transmission is also used for wireless connections between computer devices and a variety of detectors.

Intelligent haunting
A haunting of a spirit or other entity that has the ability to interact with the living and do things that can make its presence known.

Milli-gauss
Unit of measurement, measures in 1000th of a gauss and is named for the famous German mathematician, Karl Gauss.

Orbs
Anomalous spherical shapes that appear on video and still photography.

Pendulum
A pointed item hung on the end of a string or chain; it's used as a means of contacting spirits. An individual will hold the item and let it hang from the fingertips. The individual will ask questions aloud and the pendulum answers by moving.

Poltergeist haunting

A haunting that has two sides, but same kinds of activity in common. Violent outbursts of activity with doors and windows slamming shut, items being thrown across a room and things being knocked off of surfaces. Poltergeist hauntings are usually focused around a specific individual who resides or works at the location of the activity reported, and, in some cases, when the person is not present at the location, activity does not occur. A poltergeist haunting may be the cause of a human agent or spirit/energy that may be present at the location.

Portal

An opening in the realm of the paranormal that is a gateway between one dimension and the next. A passageway for spirits to come and go through. See also Vortex.

Residual haunting

A haunting that is an imprint of an event or person that plays itself out like a loop until the energy that causes it has burned itself out.

Scrying

The act of eliciting information with the use of a pendulum from spirits.

Table Tipping

A form of spirit communication, it's the act of a table being used as a form of contact. Individuals will sit around a table and lightly place their fingertips on the edge of the table and elicit contact with a spirit. The Spirit will respond by "tipping" or moving the table.

Talking Boards

A board used as a means of communicating with a spirit. Also known as a Quija Board.

Vortex

A place or situation regarded as drawing into its center all that surrounds it.

White Noise

A random noise signal that has the same sound energy level as all frequencies.

Equipment Explanations

In this section, the Chester County Paranormal Research Society looks at the application and benefits of equipment used on investigations with greater detail. The equipment used for an investigation plays a vital role in the ability to collect objective evidence and helps to determine what *is* and *is not* paranormal activity. But a key point to be made here is: the investigator is the most important tool on any investigation. With that said, let us now take a look at the main pieces of equipment used during an investigation.

The Geiger Counter

The Geiger counter is device that measures radiation. A "Geiger counter" usually contains a metal tube with a thin metal wire along its middle. The space in between them is sealed off and filled with a suitable gas and with the wire at about +1000 volts relative to the tube.

An ion or electron penetrating the tube (or an electron knocked out of the wall by X-rays or gamma rays) tears electrons off atoms in the gas. Because of the high positive voltage of the central wire, those electrons are then attracted to it. They gain energy that collide with atoms and release more electrons, until the process snowballs into an "avalanche," producing an easily detectable pulse of current. With a suitable filling gas, the flow of electricity stops by itself, or else the electrical circuitry can help stop it.

The instrument was called a "counter" because every particle passing it produced an identical pulse, allowing particles to be counted, usually electronically. But it did not tell anything about their identity or energy, except that they must have sufficient energy to penetrate the walls of the counter.

The Geiger counter is used in paranormal research to measure the background radiation at a location. The working theory in this field is that paranormal activity can effect the background radiation. In some cases, it will increase the radiation levels and in other cases it will decrease the levels.

Digital and 35mm Film Cameras

The camera is an imperative piece of equipment that enabled us to gather objective evidence during a case. Some of the best evidence presented from cases of paranormal activity over the years has been because of photographs taken. If you own your own digital camera or 35mm film camera, you need to be fully aware of what the cameras abilities and limitations are. Digital cameras have been at the center of great debate in the field of paranormal research over the years.

The earlier incarnations of digital cameras were full of inherent problems and notorious for creating "false positive" pictures. A "false positive" picture is a picture that has anomalous elements within the picture that are the result of a camera defect or other natural occurrence. There are many pictures scattered about the Internet that claim to be of true paranormal activity, but in fact they are "false positives." Orbs, defined as anomalous paranormal energy that can show up as balls of light or streaks in still photography or video, are the most controversial pictures of paranormal energy in the field. There are so many theories (good and bad) about the origin of orbs and what they are. Every picture in the CCPRS collection that has an orb—or orbs—are not presented in a way that state that they are absolutely paranormal of nature. I have yet to capture an orb photo that made me feel certain that in fact it is of a paranormal nature.

If you use your own camera, understand that your camera is vital. I encourage all members who own their own cameras to do research on the make and model of the camera and see what other consumers are saying about them. Does the manufacturer give any info regarding possible defects or design flaws with that particular model? Understanding your camera will help to rule out the possibility of interpreting a "false positive" for an authentic picture of paranormal activity.

Video Cameras

The video camera is also a fundamental tool in the investigation as another way for collecting objective evidence that can support the proof of paranormal activity. The video camera can be used in various ways during the investigation. It can be set on a tripod and left in a location where paranormal activity has been reported. It can also be used as a hand-held camera and the investigator will take it with them during their walk through investigation as a means of documenting to hopefully capture anomalous activity on tape. Infra-Red technology has become a feature on most consumer level video cameras and depending on the manufacturer can be called "night shot" or "night alive." What this technology does is allow us to use the camera in zero light. Most cameras with this feature will add a green tint or haze to the camera when it is being used in this mode. A video camera with this ability holds great appeal to the paranormal investigator.

EMF/ELF Meters

What is an EMF/ELF meter? Good question. The EMF/ELF meter is a meter that measures Electric and Magnetic fields in an AC or DC current field. It measures in a unit of measurement called "milli-gauss," named for the famous German mathematician, Karl Gauss. Most meters will measure in a range of 1-5 or 1-10 milli-gauss. The reason that EMF meters are used in paranormal research is because of the theory that a spirit or paranormal energy can add to the energy field when it is materializing or is present in a location. The theory says that, typically, an energy that measures between 3-7 milli-gauss may be of a paranormal origin. This doesn't mean that an artificial field can't also measure within this range. That is why we take base readings and make maps notating where artificial fields occur. The artificial fields are a direct result of electricity, i.e. wiring, appliances, light switches, electrical outlets, circuit breakers, high voltage power lines, sub-stations, etc.

The Earth emits a naturally occurring magnetic field all around us and has an effect on paranormal activity. Geo-magnetic storm activity can also have a great influence on paranormal activity. For more information on this kind of phenomena visit: www.noaa.sec.com.

There are many different types of EMF meters; and each one, although it measures with the same unit of measurement, may react differently. An EMF meter can range from anywhere to $12 to $1,000 or more depending on the quality and features that it has. Most meters are measuring the AC (alternating current, the type of fields created by man-made electricity) fields and some can measure DC (direct current-naturally occurring fields, batteries also fall into the category of DC) fields. The benefit of having a meter that can measure DC fields is that they will automatically filter out the artificial fields created by AC fields and can pick up more naturally occurring electro magnetic fields. Some of the higher-tech EMF meters are so sensitive that they can pick up the fields generated by living beings. The EMF meter was originally designed to measure the earth's magnetic fields and also to measure the fields created by electrical an artificial means.

There have been various studies over the years about the long-term effects of individuals living in or near high fields. There has been much controversy as to whether or not long-term exposure to high fields can lead to cancer. It has been proven though that no matter what, long term exposure to high fields can be harmful to your health. The ability to locate these high fields within a private residence or business is vital to the investigation. We may offer suggestions to the client as to possible solutions for dealing with high fields. The wiring in a home or business can greatly affect the possibility of high fields. If the wiring is old and/or not shielded correctly, it can emit high fields that may affect the ability to correctly notate any anomalous fields that may be present.

Audio Recording Equipment

Audio recording equipment is used for conducting EVP (Electronic Voice Phenomena) research and experiments. What is an EVP? An EVP is a phenomenon where paranormal voices or sounds can be captured with audio recording devices. The theory is that the activity will imprint directly onto the device or tape, but has not been proven to be an absolute fact. The use of an external microphone is essential when conducting EVP experiments with analog recording equipment. The internal microphone on an analog tape recorder can pick up the background noise of the working parts within the tape recorder and can taint the evidence as a whole. Most digital recorders are quiet enough to use the internal microphone, but as a general rule of thumb, we do not use them. An external microphone will be used always. Another theory about EVP research is that an authentic EVP will happen within the range 250-400hz. This is a lower frequency range and isn't easily heard by the human ear, and the human voice does not emit in this range. EVP is rarely heard at the moment it happens—it is usually revealed during the playback and analysis portion of the investigation.

Thermometers

The use of a thermometer in an investigation goes without saying. This is how we monitor the temperature changes during the course of an investigation. CCPRS is currently using Digital thermometers with remote sensors as a way to set up a perimeter and to notate any changes in a stationary location of an investigation. The Air-probe thermometer can take "real time" readings that are instantly accurate. This is the more appropriate thermometer for measuring air temperature and "cold spots" that may be caused by the presence of paranormal phenomena. The IR Non-contact thermometer is the most misused thermometer in the field of paranormal research. CCPRS does not own or use IR Non-contact thermometers for this reason. The IR (infra-red) Non-contact thermometer is meant for measuring surface temperatures from a remote location. It shoots an infrared beam out to an object and bounces to the unit and gives the temperature reading. I have seen, first hand, investigators using this thermometer as a way to measure air temperature. NO, this is not correct! Enough said. In an email conversation that I have had with Grant Wilson from TAPS, he has said that, "Any change in temperature that can't be measured with your hand is not worth notating..."

Bibliography

Davis, Jefferson. *A Haunted Tour Guide to the Pacific Northwest.*
Vancouver, Washington: Norseman Ventures, 2001.
Ghosts, Critters & Sacred Places of Washington and Oregon.
Vancouver, Washington: Norseman Ventures, 1999.

Helm, Mike. *Oregon's Ghosts & Monsters.* Eugene, Oregon: Rainy
Day Press, 1983.

Jenkins, Arlene. *Oregon Hauntings and the Unexplained.* Bend,
Oregon: Maverick Publications, 2002.

MacDonald, Margaret. *Ghost Stories from the Pacific Northwest.*
Little Rock, Arkansas: August House, 1995.

Nash, Tom and Scofield, Twilo. *The Well-Traveled Casket – Oregon
Folklore.* Eugene, Oregon: Meadowlark Press, 1999.

Smith, Barbara. *Ghost Stories of the Rocky Mountains Volume
II.* Auburn, Washington: Ghost House Books, 2003.

Websites:

www.theshadowlands.net/places
www.trailsendparanormalsociety.org
www.oregonparanormalsociety.com
www.bigfootencounters.com
www.stancourtney.com/squatchmarks.html
www.bfro.net
www.oregonbigfoot.com
www.oregonmufon.com
www.ghostsofamerica.com
www.thebeachconnection.net

Index